ISBN: 978129022355

Published by:
HardPress Publishing
8345 NW 66TH ST #2561
MIAMI FL 33166-2626

Email: info@hardpress.net
Web: http://www.hardpress.net

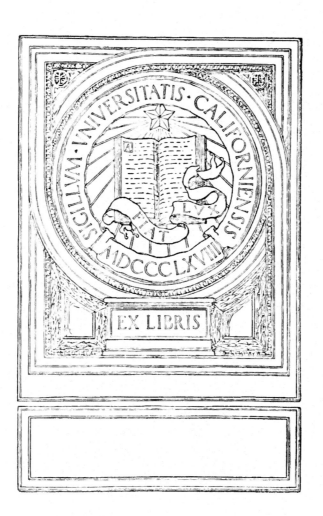

MEDICINE AND KINDRED ARTS IN THE
PLAYS OF SHAKESPEARE

Medicine & Kindred Arts
in the
Plays of Shakespeare

BY
DR. JOHN MOYES
LARGS
FELLOW OF THE FACULTY OF PHYSICIANS AND SURGEONS
GLASGOW

Glasgow
James MacLehose & Sons
Publishers to the University
1896

GLASGOW: PRINTED AT THE UNIVERSITY PRESS
BY ROBERT MACLEHOSE AND CO.

To

PROFESSOR WILLIAM TENNENT GAIRDNER
M.D., LL.D., F.R.S.

PREFACE.

THE late Dr. John Moyes presented his Thesis for the Doctorate of Medicine to Glasgow University in 1886; it was entitled "Medicine and its Kindred Arts in the Plays of Shakespeare." He had worked at the subject for years, but after the completion of the thesis, when he contemplated publishing it, he tried, if possible, to make it better. Professor Gairdner, to whom he had arranged, just before his death, to dedicate this little work, had himself read the manuscript, and had suggested that it should be revised by some recognized Shakespearean scholar; he named an old fellow student of his own, the late Dr. Brinsley Nicholson, as one who had the requisite qualifications for the work, and, at Professor Gairdner's request, that gentleman undertook the task. Numerous annotations in pencil showed the care and the knowledge he brought to bear on the subject,—knowledge both of the Shakespearean writings and of the medicine of that time. It was some guarantee of the value of this thesis that it came out of such a revision so well. Dr. Nicholson suggested that the work of "Batman uppon Bartholome his Booke *De Proprietatibus Rerum*, newly corrected, enlarged, and amended," Lond., 1582, should be carefully studied, in connection with Shakespearean medicine, as showing the notions of physiology and disease then current. Dr. Moyes found this volume in our Hunterian Library in Glasgow, and his MSS. bear evidence of extracts he had made from it. But living at a distance from Glasgow, he was unable to devote the time necessary for consulting this book in the library (as the books there are not lent out), and he regretted that he had not been able to study it sufficiently.

In working at his subject, Dr. Moyes deliberately avoided reading any attempts previously made in depicting Shakespeare's relation to medicine, as he was anxious to work out his own idea of the subject. He made up a list of books which he had used in the preparation of his Thesis; these were all calculated to throw light on the state of the profession and of medicine at the time, and this list does not contain a single essay of the kind he attempted.

The following is his list:—

JOHN COTTA [of Northampton].—A Short Discoverie of the unobserved dangers of severall sorts of ignorant and unconsiderate Practisers of Physicke in England. Lond. 1612.

[CHRISTOPHER MERRETT].—The Accomplisht Physician, the honest Apothecary, and the Skilful Chyrurgeon. London, 1670.

ROBERT GODFREY.—Various injuries and abuses in Chymical and Galenical Physick, committed both by Physicians and Apothecaries, detected. Lond. 1674.

RICHARD GRIFFITH.—A-la-Mode Phlebotomy, no good fashion. Lond. 1681.

NATHANIEL HODGES.—Vindiciae Medicinae et Medicorum. Lond. 1666.

M[ARCHMONT] N[EDHAM].—Medela Medicinae: a plea for the free profession and renovation of the Art of Physick. Lond. 1665.

RICHARD WALKER.—Memoirs of Medicine. Lond. 1799.

JOHN MASON GOOD.—History of Medicine. Lond. 1795.

SAMUEL FERRIS.—General View of . . . . Physic. Lond. 1795.

Medicina flagellata ; or The doctor scarify'd. Lond. 1721.
[Anon.]

J. M. RICHARDS.—A Chronology of Medicine, Ancient, Mediaeval, and Modern. Lond. 1880.

H. HAESER.—Lehrbuch der Geschichte der Medicin. 1875-81.

In preparing this Thesis for the press, I thought it would add to its interest and value if a pretty full bibliography of productions similar to it were appended. This I have done as well as I can, beginning with Farren in 1826; but, as stated in the list itself, I have not been able to see many of these works, and I have had to give not a few of them on the authorities there quoted.

A glance at that list shows that a very considerable part of this literature bears on the delineations of insanity in Shakespeare's plays. This was a part of the subject which Dr. Moyes decided to leave untouched, partly because there were available, amongst many others, the admirable essays of Dr. J. C. Bucknill in this country on *The Mad Folk of Shakespeare*, and partly, no doubt, because he felt that if such subjects were to be taken up at all, the authority of an expert in insanity was required to give their discussion any serious value.

Just at the time when his fatal illness seized him in December, 1894, Dr. Moyes had decided, at last, on publishing his Thesis, although he intended, I believe, to rewrite or to extend the introductory chapter. As already stated, he had obtained from Professor Gairdner his acceptance of the dedication; a portion was in proof to estimate its size, and he meant to push the work forward to a completion. A new phase of his illness, however, made it imperative that the MS. be put away from him, and so it was left imperfectly prepared.

The difficulties experienced in sending it to the press arose from some ambiguity as to how he intended to finish the introductory chapter and how to begin the next; and from doubt how far he meant to act upon some of the suggestions in Dr. Nicholson's annotations.

On surveying the various MSS., I thought it a pity to have so much careful and interesting work lost to the public view, knowing how many different kinds of people are attracted by such studies. Certain things in the MS. obviously required correction on revision for the press, but these were generally trifling. It seemed clear that even if the services of a competent editor, with adequate time, could be secured, the process of revision, if carried very far, would destroy the individuality of Dr. Moyes' work. As I had frequently been consulted on the subject of the Thesis and its publication, it seemed natural that, when leisure permitted, I should undertake the preparation of the MS. for the press, although I could not bring to the task any very special qualifications for it. I duly considered, however, all the annotations of Dr. Nicholson; when they seemed important, or when they did not imply any extensive alterations, I have usually given effect to them, just as I believe Dr. Moyes himself intended to do.

No doubt if Dr. Moyes had been resident near good libraries, or if a competent editor had undertaken to revise and annotate this work, many important suggestions might have been obtained from the numerous commentaries on Shakespeare as regards the meaning of special passages or the allusions they contain. Or again, a critical study of some of the books and papers contained in the bibliography appended might have supplied much matter for supplementary or corrective remarks. But for the reasons already stated, this was not attempted by the author, and it has not been attempted now in editing this Thesis. A few references and supplementary notes, however, have been added when these seemed desirable for the elucidation of the subject or the supplying of omissions detected in the revision.

It only remains to add that Dr. Moyes had intended to write a supplementary chapter, by way of comparison, on the medical allusions found in the writings of Marlowe and Ben Jonson; but of this a mere fragment exists in his MSS., and although an obviously important part of the subject, this must be left for other hands.

JAMES FINLAYSON, M.D.

2 WOODSIDE PLACE,
   GLASGOW, June, 1896.

CONTENTS.

	PAGE
INTRODUCTORY,	1

CHAPTER I.
PHYSIOLOGICAL AND PATHOLOGICAL NOTIONS, ... 9

CHAPTER II.
MEDICINE, ... 17

CHAPTER III.
MATERIA MEDICA, TOXICOLOGY, AND THERAPEUTICS, . . 46

CHAPTER IV.
SURGERY, ... 75
VENEREAL DISEASES, ... 86

CHAPTER V.

	PAGE
MIDWIFERY,	98
BIBLIOGRAPHY OF SHAKESPEAREAN MEDICINE,	113
INDEX,	117

MEDICINE IN SHAKESPEARE

INTRODUCTORY

THE time in which Shakespeare lived corresponded to that period in medicine which immediately preceded the discovery of the circulation of the blood. Vesalius, the great anatomist, died about a year before Shakespeare's birth; Harvey announced his discovery about ten years after Shakespeare's death. In that interval great advances were made in all branches of knowledge associated with medicine. In anatomy and physiology a few names will suffice to mark the period. Fallopius was but recently dead; Eustachius still lived; Fabricius, who discovered the valves of the veins, was teaching in Padua; Servetus entombed in a theological work a description of the pulmonary circulation; Columbus of Rome explained the relation of the pulse to the systole and diastole of the heart; and Caesalpini stood on the brink of anticipating Harvey's discovery.

In medicine the time was one of transition, and hence of strife. Galen's theories were being called in question. Early in the century the great controversy between Brissot and the Arabian school as to whether it were better to perform phlebotomy near the seat of the disease or at a distance from it had taken place, and its echoes had hardly died away. Paracelsus too had lived and taught, and the contest between his disciples and the Galenists was prolonged into the seventeenth century. The air was indeed full of the din made by contending theorists; but notwithstanding this, the medical art was advancing. In quiet nooks workers upon the Hippocratic method were placing it on a surer basis. Beside the literature of controversy are found descriptions of epidemics, works on pathological anatomy, treatises on typhus and syphilis, and carefully recorded clinical observations. There were many eminent physicians: *Guillaume de Baillou*, who has been likened to the English Sydenham; *Crato v. Krafftheim*, the pupil of Luther and Melancthon; *Schenck of Gräfenberg; Montanus*, who gave clinical instruction at the San Francesco Hospital in Padua, the first instance of such teaching being methodically given in a medical school.

The progress of surgery at this time was even more remarkable. This branch was able to profit earlier than medicine by the labours of the anatomists. Wars were frequent. Firearms were being increasingly used. Opportunities, given in this way for observation, led to more correct views as to healing, as to modes of and times for amputation, and as to prevention of bleeding. It was the era, in a word, associated surgically with the names of *Ambroise Paré* and his pupil *Guillemeau*, and with that of *Fabricius*, who gave us the trephine as we know it, and who introduced the use of the tube in tracheotomy.

In England the period followed immediately on Thomas Vicary's Mastership of the Company of Barber-Surgeons: a time when the three or four apprentices allowed to each surgeon were " clene in person and Lymm, and mete for the exercysinge of the same Mystery Science or Arte,"[1]

---

[1] South's *Memorials of the Craft of Surgery*, p. 146.

when those who were learned or could write had to bring in "an Epistell every half yere," and the unlearned who could not write or read were examined "half-yerelye what they can doo in the practyse, &c."[1]

The Royal College of Physicians had been incorporated since 1518. Three lectureships had been founded by Linacre in the Universities, two in Oxford and one in Cambridge.

The duties of the lecturers were to explain Hippocrates and Galen to the young students, and provision was made that if none in the college were capable, proper persons from any other society might be chosen. Linacre had been succeeded as president by Dr. John Caius,[2] one of the most learned men of his time, who had been a student in Padua under Montanus. Caius is said to have introduced the dissection of the human body into England, and at this time public demonstrations and dissections were held in the hall of the now united Surgeons and Barbers. Attendance at these was compulsory under fine, on every man "using the mystery or Faculty of Surgery, be he freeman, fforeyn, or alian straunger . . . being by the beadle warned thereunto."[3]

Among the arcana of Paracelsus were preparations of mercury, antimony, lead, iron, copper, arsenic, sulphur, borax, and his "laudanum." There were also tinctures and essences of plants. Extension of commerce brought into use, about this time, china root, sarsaparilla, and

---

[1] Young's *Annals of the Barber-Surgeons*, p. 310.

[2] Key : Latinized into Caius, the same who founded the College in Cambridge. Although represented in the *Dramatis personae* as a "French Physician," there is little doubt that it is he whose name is taken advantage of in the *Merry Wives of Windsor*, as "Doctor Caius."

[3] South's *Memorials of the Craft of Surgery*, p. 142.

guaiacum. But at that early stage of chemistry the composition of simple remedies even was little understood. Empirical formulas abounded. Among specifics for various diseases were crab's eyes, prepared pearls, calculous concretions, etc. There was no Pharmacopoeia. The apothecaries compounded into appropriate forms the drugs obtained from the wholesale grocer. They dealt also in wares such as snuff, tobacco, and sugar. The College of Physicians from time to time appointed four of their number who, after taking oath, inspected the apothecaries' shops to test the purity of the drugs, and with power to destroy, if necessary.

One of the features of the time was the prevalence of empiricism, nor was this to be wondered at in the state of medical knowledge. An Act of Parliament had even been passed in 1543 which conferred liberty to practise on the following comprehensive class, viz. : " Every person being the king's subject having knowledge and experience of the nature of herbs, roots, and waters, or of the operation of the same, by speculation or practice, within any part of the realm of England." Nine years later Dr. Caius enumerates as among those who practised the art : " Simple women, carpenters, pewterers, braziers, soap ball sellers, apothecaries, avaunters themselves to come from Pole, Constantinople, &c." Again in 1612, fifty years later, Cotta says : " It is a world to see what swarms abound in this kind, not only of tailors, shoemakers, weavers, midwives, cooks, and priests, but witches, conjurers, jugglers, and fortune-tellers." [1]

Many of these professed special branches, and offered to undergo examination by the Company of Barber-Surgeons. If they showed sufficient aptitude or knowledge of their

---

[1] Cotta : *Short Discoverie*, etc., p. 36.

specialism, they received a licence to practise for a longer or shorter time. Thus we read that "James Vanotten and Nicholos Bowlden are . . . permitted to practize for the couchinge of the Catarack, cuttinge for the rupture, stone, and wenne," for the space of three months; another is permitted, in addition, to cut for the wry neck and the harelip. Permission is given to "Edward Stutfeyld, a practicalner in bone settinge," to "Josper Johnson, practicalner in the Cure of a fistula," and to "John of Mounepilier, in ffrance," to practise for three months, provided "they hang not oute their banners or other shewes and signes of their profession in any other place then at the howse where they shall from tyme to tyme lye." [1]

In the pages of Shakespeare these different types of practitioners are represented. The physician in *King Lear*, the doctors in *Macbeth*, Gerard de Narbon in *All's Well*, and Dr. Butts in *Henry VIII.* represent the higher grade of the legally qualified physicians. The surgeon is often sent for when wounds have been inflicted, and a grave imputation is thrown upon his habits in the passage:

Sir To. That's all one; he has hurt me, and there's the end on't. Sot, didst see Dick surgeon, sot?
Clo. O, he's drunk, Sir Toby, an hour agone; his eyes were set at eight i' the morning.   *Twelfth Night*, v. 1.

The apothecary stands forth in all the poverty of his surroundings in *Romeo and Juliet*:

> I do remember an apothecary,—
> And hereabouts he dwells,—whom late I noted
> In tatter'd weeds, with overwhelming brows,
> Culling of simples; meagre were his looks,
> Sharp misery had worn him to the bones;

---

[1] South's *Memorials of the Craft of Surgery*, p. 161.

> And in his needy shop a tortoise hung,
> An alligator stuff'd, and other skins
> Of ill-shaped fishes ; and about his shelves
> A beggarly account of empty boxes,
> Green earthen pots, bladders and musty seeds,
> Remnants of packthread, and old cakes of roses,
> Were thinly scatter'd, to make up a show.
> *Romeo and Juliet,* v. 1.

And the class of whom Cotta complains furnishes Pinch the conjurer in the *Comedy of Errors*:

> They brought one Pinch, a hungry lean-faced villain,
> A mere anatomy, a mountebank,
> A thread-bare juggler, and a fortune-teller ;
> A needy, hollow-ey'd, sharp looking wretch,
> A living-dead man : this pernicious slave
> Forsooth, took on him as a conjurer ;
> And, gazing in mine eyes, feeling my pulse,
> And with no face, as t'were, outfacing me,
> Cries out, I was possessed. *Comedy of Errors,* v. 1.

Various passages show, moreover, that Shakespeare was not unacquainted with the rival schools of medicine and with the great medical names of antiquity.

That he was acquainted with the controversy between the Galenists and the chemists we learn from the passage in *All's Well that Ends Well,* where Lafeu speaks of the king as " relinquished of the artists," and Parolles replies, " so I say ; both of Galen and Paracelsus." The following is the passage :

Laf. They say, miracles are past ; and we have our philosophical persons, to make modern and familiar, things supernatural and causeless. Hence is it, that we make trifles of terrors ; ensconcing ourselves into seeming knowledge, when we should submit ourselves to an unknown fear.

Par. Why, 'tis the rarest argument of wonder, that hath shot out in our latter times.

Ber. And so 'tis.
Laf. To be relinquished of the artists,—
Par. So I say; both of Galen and Paracelsus.
Laf. Of all the learned and authentic fellows,—
Par. Right, so I say.
Laf. That gave him out incurable,—
Par. Why, there 'tis; so say I too.
Laf. Not to be helped,—
Par. Right; as 'twere a man assured of an—
Laf. Uncertain life, and sure death.
All's Well that Ends Well, ii. 3.

The occurrence of the names of Galen and Paracelsus in this connection is not fortuitous; the meaning is that neither the old sect who swore by Galen nor the chemists who pinned their faith to Paracelsus could render the king any help. This view is strengthened by the word "schools" occurring in a previous part of the same play:

How shall they credit
A poor unlearned virgin, when the schools
Embowell'd of their doctrine, have left off
The danger to itself?

All's Well that Ends Well, i. 3.

The above is the only mention of Paracelsus, but in the *Merry Wives of Windsor* (ii. 3; iii. 1), the names of Esculapius, Hippocrates, and Galen appear. Esculapius appears also in *Pericles* (iii. 2), and in the second part of *Henry IV*. Falstaff in the following passage, while discoursing of apoplexy, claims to have derived his knowledge of it from Galen:

Fal. And I hear, moreover, his highness is fallen into this same whoreson apoplexy.
Ch. Just. Well, Heaven mend him! I pray, let me speak with you.

Fal. This apoplexy is, as I take it, a kind of lethargy, an't please your lordship; a kind of sleeping in the blood, a whoreson tingling.

Ch. Just. What tell you me of it? be it as it is.

Fal. It has its original from much grief; from study, and perturbation of the brain; I have read the cause of its effects in Galen; it is a kind of deafness.   *II. Henry IV.* i. 2.

The name of Galen also occurs in *Coriolanus*:

Men. A letter for me? It gives me an estate of seven years' health; in which time I will make a lip at the physician: the most sovereign prescription in Galen is but empiricutic, and, to this preservative, of no better report than a horse-drench.

Coriolanus, ii. 1.

CHAPTER I

PHYSIOLOGICAL AND PATHOLOGICAL NOTIONS

IT is evident that notwithstanding the frequent references in Shakespeare to the circulation of the blood, he had no notion of its course, as understood since the discovery of Harvey. Obscure allusions suggestive of the idea of the circulation of blood, *when we have this in our mind*, do occur:

> *Bru.* You are my true and honourable wife;
> As dear to me as are the ruddy drops
> Which visit my sad heart. *Julius Caesar*, ii. 1.

Or, again, in a passage to be subsequently quoted in connection with Death (p. 42), where he speaks of the blood, at death, going to the heart:

> Which with the heart there cools and ne'er returneth
> To blush and beautify the cheek again.
> *II. Henry VI.* iii. 2.

Bartholomaeus, in 1366, speaks of the running of blood in the veins and the running of blood and air (vital spirits) in the arteries.

The famous metaphor in *Coriolanus*, where the senators of Rome are likened to the belly, and the mutinous citizens to the other members of the body rebelling against it, furnishes us with a good general view of digestion and nutrition.[1] It also refers to sending rivers

of blood
Even to the court, the heart.

Men. There was a time, when all the body's members
Rebell'd against the belly ; thus accused it :
That only like a gulf it did remain
I' the midst o' the body, idle and inactive,
Still cupboarding the viand, never bearing
Like labour with the rest, where the other instruments
Did see, and hear, devise, instruct, walk, feel,
And, mutually participate, did minister
Unto the appetite and affection common
Of the whole body. The belly answered,—
  First Cit. Well, sir, what answer made the belly ?

. . . .

  Men. . . . .
' True is it, my incorporate friends,' quoth he,
' That I receive the general food at first,
Which you do live upon ; and fit it is,
Because I am the store-house, and the shop
Of the whole body : But, if you do remember,
I send it through the rivers of your blood,
Even to the court, the heart,—to the seat o' the brain ;
And, through the cranks and offices of man,
The strongest nerves, and small inferior veins
From me receive that natural competency
Whereby they live : And though that all at once,
You, my good friends' (this says the belly), mark me,—
  First Cit. Ay, sir ; well, well.

---

[1] In "Batman uppon Bartholome his Booke *De proprietatibus rerum*," Book v., chapter 38, we read : "The stomach is the purveyor and husband of all the body, and the stomach taketh feeding for all the members and serveth all the members thereof as it needeth, as saith Constantine." This was published in London in 1582. It is evidently the same idea which Shakespeare amplifies.

> *Men.* 'Though all at once cannot
> See what I do deliver out to each:
> Yet I can make my audit up, that all
> From me do back receive the flour of all,
> And leave me but the bran.' What say you to 't?
> *Coriolanus*, i. 1.

The following passage also bears upon nutrition and its relation to the blood and veins:

> he had not dined:
> The veins unfill'd, our blood is cold, and then
> We pout upon the morning, are unapt
> To give or to forgive; but, when we have stuff'd
> These pipes and these conveyances of our blood
> With wine and feeding, we have suppler souls
> Than in our priest-like fasts; therefore I'll watch him
> Till he be dieted to my request,
> And then I'll set upon him. *Coriolanus*, v. 1.

The beliefs of Hippocrates that the liver was the great organ of blood-making, and that it had also a faculty of generating heat, throw light upon many of the passages where the mention of this organ occurs. Thus, Sir Toby Belch in *Twelfth Night* says:

> For Andrew, if he were opened, and you find so much blood in his liver as will clog the foot of a flea, I'll eat the rest of the anatomy.
> *Twelfth Night*, iii. 2.

Bearing on white livers and cowardice, we have the following:

> How many cowards, whose hearts are all as false
> As stairs of sand, wear yet upon their chins
> The beards of Hercules, and frowning Mars;
> Who, inward search'd, have livers white as milk!
> *Merchant of Venice*, iii. 2.

For "lily-livered" in this sense, see also *Macbeth*, v. 3, and *King Lear*, ii. 2.

The effect of wine in improving the liver and the courage is insisted on by Falstaff:

The second property of your excellent sherris is,—the warming of the blood; which, before cold and settled, left the liver white and pale, which is the badge of pusillanimity and cowardice; but the sherris warms it, and makes it course from the inwards to the parts extreme. *II. Henry IV*. iv. 3.

Falstaff, discoursing further of the effect of sherris, makes coldness of blood synonymous with cowardice, and heat of blood with valour:

Prince Harry is valiant; for the cold blood he did naturally inherit of his father, he hath, like lean, sterile, and bare land, manured, husbanded, and tilled, with excellent endeavour of drinking good, and good store of fertile sherris; that he is become very hot and valiant. If I had a thousand sons, the first human principle I would teach them, should be,—to forswear thin potations, and addict themselves to sack. *II. Henry IV*. iv. 3.

Just before, in the same speech, he ascribes the pallor of the liver to the coldness of the blood, and in particular he says, "the sherris warms it and *makes it course from the inwards to the parts extreme.*"

Again,

reason and respect
Make livers pale, and lustihood deject.
Troilus and Cressida, ii. 2.

You, that are old, consider not the capacities of us that are young: you measure the heat of our livers with the bitterness of your galls; and we, that are in the vaward of our youth, I must confess, are wags too. *II. Henry IV*. i. 2.

Two other passages agree with the statement of Falstaff that drinking warmed the blood in the liver, viz:

Char. I had rather heat my liver with drinking.
Antony and Cleopatra, i. 2.

> And let my liver rather heat with wine,
> Than my heart cool with mortifying groans.
> Why should a man, whose blood is warm within,
> Sit like his grandsire cut in alabaster?
> Sleep, when he wakes? and creep into the jaundice
> By being peevish? *Merchant of Venice*, i. 1.

The other references to this organ are in passages where the love of the sexes is spoken of, and no doubt their explanation, also, is to be found in its two supposed functions above spoken of; but the connection of the liver with love was a tradition from classical times:

> The white-cold virgin snow upon my heart
> Abates the ardour of my liver. *Tempest*, iv. 1.

The *pia mater* is referred to three times in the plays. The most important of these allusions is the following:

> *Hol.* This is a gift that I have, simple, simple; a foolish extravagant spirit, full of forms, figures, shapes, objects, ideas, apprehensions, motions, revolutions; these are begot in the ventricle of memory, nourished in the womb of *pia mater*, and delivered upon the mellowing of occasion. *Love's Labour's Lost*, iv. 2.

In the other passages, *pia mater* seems to be used simply as meaning the brain; "a most weak *pia mater*" (*Twelfth Night*, i. 5); "his *pia mater* is not worth the ninth part of a sparrow" (*Troilus and Cressida*, ii. 1). The use of the term *pia mater*, for the soft membrane in contact with the brain, arose from the notion that the brain was not merely nourished by the membranes, but actually *formed* from them, ideas well indicated by the phrase "nourished in the womb of *pia mater*." Sir B. W. Richardson, in a paper noted in the Bibliography, supposes that Shakespeare may have seen the sheets or drawings of Crooke's *Microcosmographia*, London, 1616 (Pref. dated 1615), a large folio which was printed by W. Jaggard, whose place of business would be well known to Shakespeare, as he had printed things for him also. The value of this suggestion will depend on the dates of the Plays where the phrase occurs.

Regarding the "ventricle of memory," the following extract from Vicary's *Anatomie of the Bodie of Man*, issued in 1548 (Early Text Society, 1888, Extra Series, liii., p. 31) may be quoted. In the margin, we read: "In the foremost Ventricle are the Five Wits: also the Fancy and the Imagination. In the 2nd or middle Ventricle is Thought. In the 3rd Ventricle is the Memory." In the text, we read: "In the 3rd Ventrikle, and last, there is founded and ordeyned the vertue Memoratiue: in this place is registred and kept those things that are done and spoken with the senses," etc., etc.

It is of some importance to notice how familiarly acquainted Shakespeare was with the two leading pathological doctrines of the ancients, viz., that of the "vital spirits," which dwelt in the arteries, and that other doctrine of "humours," which still lingers in popular belief and even now forms the basis of some so-called systems of cure:

> Why, universal plodding prisons up
> The nimble spirits in the arteries;
> As motion, and long-during action, tires
> The sinewy vigour of the traveller.
> *Love's Labour's Lost*, iv. 3.

> Take thou this phial, being then in bed,
> And this distilled liquor drink thou off:
> When, presently through all thy veins shall run
> A cold and drowsy humour, which shall seize
> Each vital spirit. *Romeo and Juliet*, iv. 1.

The next two quotations should be read also in connection with the two passages previously quoted (pp. 9, 10) as to the circulation of the blood:

> Or if that surly spirit, melancholy,
> Had baked thy blood, and made it heavy, thick;

(Which else, runs tickling up and down the veins,
Making that idiot, laughter, keep men's eyes,
And strain their cheeks to idle merriment,
A passion hateful to my purposes).   *King John*, iii. 3.

and it cannot be,
That, whiles warm life plays in that infant's veins.
Ibid. iii. 4.

In the following passages the word "Humours" has, without question, a pathological significance. It might indeed bear this interpretation in many other places where it occurs as, *e.g.* where Desdemona says, "Methinks the sun where he was born drew all such humours from him" (*Othello*, iii. 4), but only those passages have been taken where no question can be raised as to the meaning:

I

Do come with words as med'cinal as true,
Honest as either, to purge him of that humour
That presses him from sleep.   *Winter's Tale*, ii. 3.

King. So it is, besieged with sable-coloured melancholy, I did commend the black-oppressing humour to the most wholesome physic of thy health-giving air; and, as I am a gentleman, betook myself to walk.   *Love's Labour's Lost*, i. 1.

D. *Pedro.* What! sigh for the toothache?
Leon. Where is but a humour, or a worm!
Much Ado About Nothing, iii. 2.

Nym. The king hath run bad humours on the knight, that's the even of it.
Pist. Nym, thou hast spoke the right;
His heart is fracted, and corroborate.
Nym. The king is a good king: but it must be as it may; he passes some humours and careers.   *Henry V.* ii. 1.

Why dost thou converse with that trunk of humours, that bolting-hutch of beastliness, that swoln parcel of dropsies, that huge bombard of sack, that stuffed cloak-bag of guts, that roasted Manningtree ox with the pudding in his belly, that reverend vice, that grey iniquity, that father ruffian, that vanity in years?
I. Henry IV. ii. 4.

> This inundation of mistemper'd humour
> Rests by you only to be qualified.
> Then pause not ; for the present time's so sick,
> That present medicine must be minister'd,
> Or overthrow incurable ensues. *King John*, v. 1.

Closely allied to "Humours" are the "Rheums" or Catarrhal fluxes, of which also we find frequent mention :

> Is not your father grown incapable
> Of reasonable affairs ? is he not stupid
> With age, and altering rheums ? Can he speak ? hear ?
> Know man from man ? dispute his own estate ?
> Lies he not bed-rid ? and again does nothing.
> But what he did being childish ? *Winter's Tale*, iv. 3.

> And death unloads thee : Friend hast thou none ;
> For thine own bowels, which do call thee sire,
> The mere effusion of thy proper loins,
> Do curse the gout, serpigo, and the rheum,
> For ending thee no sooner.
> *Measure for Measure*, iii. 1.

> *Eno.* That year, indeed, he was troubled with a rheum.
> *Antony and Cleopatra*, iii. 2.

> You say so :
> You that did void your rheum upon my beard,
> And foot me, as you spurn a stranger cur
> Over your threshold ; monies is your suit.
> *Merchant of Venice*, i. 3.

Ant. S. Where England ?
Dro. S. I looked for the chalky cliffs, but I could find no whiteness in them ; but I guess, it stood in her chin, by the salt rheum that ran between France and it. *Comedy of Errors*, iii. 2.

Oth. I have a salt and sullen rheum offends me :
Lend me thy handkerchief. *Othello*, iii. 4.

The pathological doctrine of "obstructions" current in Shakespeare's time is referred to at page 68.

CHAPTER II

MEDICINE

THE diseases of which most frequent mention is made are: AGUE, RHEUMATISM, PLAGUES and PESTILENCES, FEVERS, MEAZELS, THE SWEAT, LEPROSY.

Among others which receive casual mention are: APOPLEXY, BONEACHE, COLIC, CONSUMPTION, CONVULSIONS, CRAMPS, DROPSY, ECSTASY, EPILEPSY, GOUT, GREEN SICKNESS, HEARTBURN, HEMIPLEGIA, HYDROPHOBIA, ITCH, JAUNDICE, PALSY, SCIATICA, SEA-SICKNESS, SOMNAMBULISM, TETTER, VISUAL SPECTRA.

To these may be added the list given by Thersites in *Troilus and Cressida*; but it includes surgical as well as medical ailments, and seems to have special reference to the complications of syphilis:

> Now the rotten diseases of the south, the guts-griping, ruptures, catarrhs, loads o' gravel i' the back, lethargies, cold palsies, raw eyes, dirt-rotten livers, wheezing lungs, bladders full of imposthume, sciaticas, limekilns i' the palm, incurable bone-ache, and the rivelled fee-simple of the tetter, take and take again such preposterous discoveries! *Troilus and Cressida,* v. 1.

AGUE. This disease was much more frequent at that time than now; and its destructive influence on troops is relied on by Macbeth:

> *Macb.* Hang out our banners on the outward walls;
> The cry is still, 'They come:' Our castle's strength

> Will laugh a siege to scorn: here let them lie,
> Till famine, and the ague, eat them up.   *Macbeth*, v. 5.

Its type was also more severe, and a fatal result from it more common. It causes the death of John of Gaunt in the second act of *Richard II.*

When Cassius instigates Brutus against Caesar, he describes a fever which Caesar had in Spain. The following is the passage, and the severe rigor, the pallor of the lips, the dulness of the eye, the thirst, and the weakness identify the illness with an attack of ague:

> He had a fever when he was in Spain,
> And, when the fit was on him, I did mark
> How he did shake: 'tis true, this god did shake,
> His coward lips did from their colour fly;
> And that same eye, whose bend doth awe the world,
> Did lose his lustre: I did hear him groan:
> Ay, and that tongue of his, that bade the Romans
> Mark him, and write his speeches in their books,
> Alas! it cried, 'Give me some drink, Titinius,'
> As a sick girl.   *Julius Caesar*, i. 2.

The most characteristic symptom of ague, viz. the shivering, is alluded to in the following passages, as also its similarity to the shaking due to fear:

> This ague-fit of fear is over-blown.   *Richard II.* iii. 2.

> Although, I know, you'll swear, terribly swear,
> Into strong shudders, and to heavenly agues,
> The immortal gods that hear you,—spare your oaths.
>   *Timon of Athens*, iv. 3.

> *Salar.* My wind, cooling my broth,
> Would blow me to an ague, when I thought
> What harm a wind too great might do at sea.
>   *Merchant of Venice*, i. 1.

In the following passage from the *Tempest* the interest lies in the allusion to delirium during the fit:

Ste. This is some monster of the isle, with four legs; who hath got, I take it, an ague: Where the devil should he learn our language? I will give him some relief, if it be but for that: If I can recover him, and keep him tame, and get to Naples with him, he's a present for any emperor that ever trod on neat's-leather.

Cal. Do not torment me, pr'ythee; I'll bring my wood home faster.

Ste. He's in his fit now; and does not talk after the wisest. He shall taste of my bottle: if he have never drunk wine afore, it will go near to remove his fit. If I can recover him, and keep him tame, I will not take too much for him: he shall pay for him that hath him, and that soundly. *Tempest*, ii. 2.

Two varieties of the disease are recognized, the quotidian and the tertian. Thus Rosalind, in *As You Like It*, says:

If I could meet that fancy-monger, I would give him some good counsel, for he seems to have the quotidian of love upon him.
As You Like It, iii. 2.

Dame Quickly, to impress the greater gravity of Sir John's illness upon her hearers, uses in a confused way the two in conjunction:

Hostess. As ever you came of women, come in quickly to Sir John: Ah, poor heart! he is so shaked of a burning quotidian tertian, that it is most lamentable to behold. Sweet men, come to him.
Henry V. ii. 1.

The action of the hot sun upon moist ground as a factor in the production of the disease was known to Shakespeare, as we learn from the passage:

Hot. No more, no more; worse than the sun in March,
This praise doth nourish agues. Let them come.
I. Henry IV. iv. 1.

Again, we have the passage in *Troilus and Cressida*:

Patr. O, then beware;
Those wounds heal ill, that men do give themselves:
Omission to do what is necessary

> Seals a commission to a blank of danger;
> And danger, like an ague, subtly taints
> Even then when we sit idly in the sun.
> *Troilus and Cressida*, iii. 3.

This may refer to the same subtle influence, or it may possibly allude to the well-known fact that in one subject to a malarial taint, the hot stage may be brought on by exposure to the sun.

The after-effects of the disease are seen in Caius Ligarius; Caesar says:

> Good-morrow, Casca.—Caius Ligarius,
> Caesar was ne'er so much your enemy,
> As that same ague which hath made you lean.
> *Julius Caesar*, ii. 2.

The physiognomy during an attack furnishes the following metaphor:

> But now will canker-sorrow eat my bud,
> And chase the native beauty from his cheek,
> And he will look as hollow as a ghost,
> As dim and meagre as an ague's fit;
> And so he'll die. *King John*, iii. 4.

The following passages have a general bearing upon the causes of MALARIAL AND RHEUMATIC DISEASES. These are ascribed very much to the same influences which at the present day we recognize as producing them:

> *Lear.* You nimble lightnings, dart your blinding flames
> Into her scornful eyes! Infect her beauty,
> You fen-suck'd fogs, drawn by the powerful sun,
> To fall and blast her pride! *King Lear*, ii. 4.

> To dare the vile contagion of the night?
> And tempt the rheumy and unpurged air
> To add unto his sickness? No, my Brutus.
> *Julius Caesar*, ii. 1.

> *Page.* And youthful still, in your doublet and hose, this raw rheumatic day? *Merry Wives of Windsor*, iii. 1.

> *Cal.* All the infections that the sun sucks up
> From bogs, fens, flats, on Prosper fall, and make him
> By inch-meal a disease! His spirits hear me.
> *Tempest*, ii. 2.

> Therefore the moon, the governess of floods,
> Pale in her anger, washes all the air,
> That rheumatic diseases do abound.
> *Midsummer-Night's Dream*, ii. 1.

Other passages referring to rheumatism are quoted below:

> *Host.* By my troth, this is the old fashion; you two never meet, but you fall to some discord: you are both, in good troth, as rheumatic as two dry toasts; you cannot one bear with another's confirmities. *II. Henry IV.* ii. 4

> *Apem.* So, so; there:—
> Aches contract and starve your supple joints!
> *Timon of Athens*, i. 1.

The frequent allusions to PLAGUES AND PESTILENCES are readily understood when it is remembered that the century in which Shakespeare lived was one remarkable for the frequency and force of its epidemics. Of their specific nature he says nothing, and only in one instance can the nature of the disease be conjectured. It is the "red pestilence," or "red plague," twice alluded to:

> *Vol.* Now the red pestilence strike all trades in Rome,
> And occupations perish! *Coriolanus*, iv. 1.

> *Cal.* You taught me language; and my profit on't
> Is, I know how to curse: The red-plague rid you,
> For learning me your language! *Tempest*, i. 2.

This was doubtless typhus fever. The disease was common at the time, and in France the name given to it was *La pourpre*, from the red eruption which accompanied it. Some have made out the reference to be to one form of the plague, but the resemblance (if not relationship) between the plague and typhus is at times so close that a celebrated physician from Egypt, seeing certain typhus fever cases in London, said that if seen at home they would have been regarded as the Plague (Murchison, *Continued Fevers*, 3rd edition, p. 220).

Occasionally Shakespeare ascribes these plagues to stellar influences :

> *Biron.* Thus pour the stars down plagues for perjury.
> *Love's Labour's Lost,* v. 2.

But in another remarkable passage he shows that he knew well the conditions under which they broke out :

> And draw their honours reeking up to heaven ;
> Leaving their earthly parts to choke your clime,
> The smell whereof shall breed a plague in France.
> Mark then abounding valour in our English.
> *Henry V.* iv. 3.

The infectiousness of disease supplies these fine metaphors :

It is certain, that either wise bearing, or ignorant carriage, is caught, as men take diseases, one of another; therefore, let men take heed of their company. *II. Henry IV.* v. 1.

> Sickness is catching ; O, were favour so !
> Yours would I catch, fair Hermia, ere I go.
> *Midsummer-Night's Dream,* i. 1.

Further allusions to infection and contagion are found in the following :

> *Sands.* 'Tis time to give them physic, their diseases
> Are grown so catching. *Henry VIII.* i. 3.

> *Mar.* All the contagion of the south light on you,
> You shames of Rome ! you herd of— Boils and plagues
> Plaster you o'er ; that you may be abhorr'd
> Farther than seen, and one infect another
> Against the wind a mile ! You souls of geese.
> *Coriolanus,* i. 4.

Beatrice turns the same idea to humorous account when she says:

> *Beat.* O Lord! he will hang upon him like a disease: he is sooner caught than the pestilence, and the taker runs presently mad. God help the noble Claudio! if he have caught the Benedick, it will cost him a thousand pound ere he be cured.
> *Much Ado About Nothing*, i. 1.

FEVERS.[1] The clinical features of fever which occur in the Plays are shivering, increased rapidity of the pulse, rise of temperature, the crisis before recovery, the weakness during convalescence, and delirium. The shivering furnishes certain metaphors:

> Thou mad'st thine enemies shake, as if the world
> Were feverous, and did tremble. *Coriolanus*, i. 4.

>   The obscure bird
> Clamour'd the live-long night: some say, the earth
> Was feverous, and did shake. *Macbeth*, ii. 3.

> The white hand of a lady fever thee,
> Shake thou to look on't.—Get thee back to Caesar.
> *Antony and Cleopatra*, iii. 11 (or 13).

> And now, instead of bullets wrapp'd in fire,
> To make a shaking fever in your walls,
> They shoot but calm words, folded up in smoke,
> To make a faithless error in your ears.
> *King John*, ii. 1.

Acceleration of the pulse in fever is referred to, where Troilus says:

> *Tro.* Even such a passion doth embrace my bosom:
> My heart beats thicker than a feverous pulse.
> *Troilus and Cressida*, iii. 2.

---

[1] See also Ague and Pestilence already mentioned.

The increase of temperature is indicated in the following:

> We are all diseased;
> And with our surfeiting and wanton hours
> Have brought ourselves into a burning fever,
> And we must bleed for it. *II. Henry IV*. iv. 1.

The crisis, or rather the precritical exacerbation of the fever, is applied metaphorically in this passage:

> *Pand.* Before the curing of a strong disease,
> Even in the instant of repair and health,
> The fit is strongest; evils, that take leave,
> On their departure most of all show evil:
> What have you lost by losing of this day?
> *King John*, iii. 4.

The fictitious strength in the delirium of fever is well described in the following comparison:

> And as the wretch, whose fever-weaken'd joints,
> Like strengthless hinges, buckle under life,
> Impatient of his fit, breaks like a fire
> Out of his keeper's arms; even so my limbs,
> Weaken'd with grief, being now enraged with grief,
> Are thrice themselves. *II. Henry IV*. i. 1.

That Shakespeare had closely observed the wanderings of the mind in illness is evident, when we study the death-bed scenes of King John and Falstaff. That of King John will be further spoken of, by and by, but here it will be convenient to notice the delirium before death. Prince Henry describes it in these terms:

> *P. Hen.* It is too late; the life of all his blood
> Is touch'd corruptibly; and his pure brain
> (Which some suppose the soul's frail dwelling-house)
> Doth, by the idle comments that it makes,
> Foretell the ending of mortality. *King John*, v. 7.

And in the speech almost immediately following:

> *P. Hen.* O vanity of sickness! fierce extremes,
> In their continuance, will not feel themselves.

> Death, having prey'd upon the outward parts,
> Leaves them insensible; and his siege is now
> Against the mind, the which he pricks and wounds
> With many legions of strange fantasies;
> Which, in their throng and press to that last hold,
> Confound themselves. 'Tis strange, that death should sing.—
> I am the cygnet to this pale faint swan,
> Who chants a doleful hymn to his own death;
> And, from the organ-pipe of frailty, sings
> His soul and body to their lasting rest. *King John*, v. 7.

The delirium here is acute and in keeping with the circumstances. The patient rages, sings, demands to be carried into the open air: contrast it with the wandering of Falstaff's mind at the close of his life, as described by Dame Quickly:

> *Quick.* Nay, sure, he's not in hell; he's in Arthur's bosom, if ever man went to Arthur's bosom. A' made a finer end, and went away, an it had been any christom child; a' parted even just between twelve and one, e'en at turning o' the tide; for after I saw him fumble with the sheets, and play with flowers, and smile upon his fingers' ends, I knew there was but one way: for his nose was as sharp as a pen, and a' babbled of green fields. How now, Sir John? quoth I: what, man, be of good cheer. So a' cried out—God, God, God! three or four times. Now I, to comfort him, bid him, a' should not think of God; I hoped there was no need to trouble himself with any such thoughts yet: So, a' bade me lay more clothes on his feet: I put my hand into the bed and felt them, and they were as cold as any stone; then I felt to his knees, and so upward and upward, and all was as cold as any stone. *Henry V.* ii. 3.

There is a reference here to the superstition not long gone out that one died about the turning of the tide. (See *New Shakespeare Society Transactions* for 1880-82, pp. 212 and 218.)

The clinical accuracy of this description requires no comment, but note the difference between the delirium of King John and that of old Sir John, who, dying in advanced life and of a long-standing ailment, "fumbled with the sheets, played with flowers, and smiled upon his fingers' ends." The gravity of the symptom is recognized in each case. "It is too late," says Prince Henry; "I knew there was but one way," says Dame Quickly, "for his nose was as sharp as a pen, and a' babbled of green fields"[1]—that he had known in his youth.

MEASLES. Coriolanus, when urged to speak in conciliatory terms to the populace, gives utterance to the following:

> *Cor.* How! no more!
> As for my country I have shed my blood,
> Not fearing outward force, so shall my lungs
> Coin words till their decay against those meazels,
> Which we disdain should tetter us, yet sought
> The very way to catch them.   *Coriolanus*, iii. 1.

The exact meaning of "Meazels," its spelling, and its relationship to leprosy, elephantiasis, smallpox, and our present-day measles constitute a very confused subject. The infectious nature of the disease, however, is clearly implied. According to Creighton, a word "meseles" is used in the poem *Piers Plowman,* meaning lepers, but John of Gaddesden uses the word "mesles" in his description of "Morbilli" (or our present-day measles). Again, "Ye Maysilles" is given in Levins' *Manipulus Vocabulorum* as meaning "Variolae" (our present-day smallpox), and in Baret's dictionary the word measles is defined as "a disease with many reddish spottes or speckles in the face and bodie,

---

[1] See, however, a different view and a different reading, urged with great ingenuity by Dr. C. Creighton, "Death of Falstaff," *Blackwood's Magazine*, March, 1889, where he suggests that his death was due to the sweating sickness, and where he advocates a different reading of this disputed passage.

much like freckles in colour." It must be remembered that the confusion was not merely one of words and names, but that smallpox (variola) and measles (morbilli) were constantly confused, and their distinction was due to the Arabian physicians and made known in England by John of Gaddesden. We may fairly suppose that "meazels" in the text refers to our present-day measles. (See Creighton's *History of Epidemics in Britain*, Vol. I., pp. 445-451, and Vol. II., p. 632 ; see also article "Measles," in Skeat's *Etymological Dictionary*, larger edition.)

SWEATING SICKNESS, called also THE SWEAT, was prevalent before Shakespeare's time in England, and Dr. Caius had written a treatise on it. As stated in the last footnote, it has been attempted to be shown that Falstaff died of this disease. The passage in *Measure for Measure*, here quoted, has been supposed to indicate the Sweating Sickness, but Creighton in his *History of Epidemics*, Vol. I., p. 413, suggests that the hot agues and fevers of the Elizabethan period often took on a sweating character, which might be confused with it :

Mrs. Ov. Thus, what with the war, what with the sweat, what with the gallows, and what with poverty, I am custom-shrunk.
Measure for Measure, i. 2.

LEPROSY. It has been supposed by some that *Meazels*, just spoken of, may have been intended to indicate Leprosy, or some form of Elephantiasis.

Mere allusions to Leprosy occur in the following passages :

I am no loathsome leper. *II. Henry VI.* iii. 2.

Speaking of the tempting power of gold, Timon says it will

Make the hoar leprosy adored. *Timon of Athens,* iv. 3.

"The leperous distilment" in the poison in *Hamlet* will be referred to subsequently, pp. 56, 57.

THE TETTER is referred to as an eruption from the contagious "*Meazels*" already mentioned (p. 26, *Coriolanus*, iii. 1); and in the list of diseases in *Troilus and Cressida*, v. 1 (see p. 17).

The effect of "the leperous distilment" in *Hamlet* is said to have brought about a tetter and a lazar-like crust.

> And a most instant tetter bark'd about,
> Most lazar-like, with vile and loathsome crust,
> All my smooth body. *Hamlet*, i. 5.

EPILEPSY. Two of Shakespeare's notable characters, Caesar and Othello, are the subjects of epilepsy. Each has an attack when presumably under the influence of the most powerful emotions. Caesar's attack is described by Casca.

> *Cas.* But, soft, I pray you : What? Did Caesar swoon?
> *Casca.* He fell down in the market-place, and foamed at mouth, and was speechless.
> *Bru.* 'Tis very like : he hath the falling-sickness.
> *Cas.* No, Caesar hath it not ; but you, and I,
> And honest Casca, we have the falling-sickness.
> *Casca.* I know not what you mean by that ; but, I am sure, Caesar fell down. If the tag-rag people did not clap him and hiss him, according as he pleased, and displeased them, as they use to do the players in the theatre, I am no true man.
> *Julius Caesar*, i. 2.

It happens when the crown, proffered by Mark Antony, has been twice refused by him amid the plaudits of the people.

The confusion of mind, which often follows an epileptic fit, is indicated in Caesar's case by Casca's narrating that

> When he came to himself again, he said, If he had done or said anything amiss, he desired their worships to think it was his infirmity. *Julius Caesar*, i. 2.

Othello's fit is described in Act iv. Sc. 1 :

> *Cas.* What is the matter ?
> *Iago.* My lord has fallen into an epilepsy :
> This is his second fit ; he had one yesterday.
> *Cas.* Rub him about the temples.
> *Iago.* No, forbear :
> The lethargy must have his quiet course :
> If not, he foams at mouth ; and, by and by,
> Breaks out to savage madness.   Look, he stirs :
> Do you withdraw yourself a little while,
> He will recover straight ; when he is gone,
> I would on great occasion speak with you.—   [*Exit Cassio.*
> How is it, general ? have you not hurt your head ?
> *Othello*, iv. 1.

The points worthy of notice here are the mental confusion preceding the fall, as seen in Othello's utterances ; the premonition of the seizure—" It is not words that shake me thus," he says ; the likelihood of injury from the sudden fall ; and, most important of all, the fit of insanity likely to follow if the lethargy was not allowed to have its " quiet course " (Post-epileptic mania).

SCIATICA.   The seat of this disease, and perhaps its dependence on syphilis, are indicated in *Measure for Measure*.

> *First Gent.* How now ! which of your hips has the most profound sciatica? *Measure for Measure*, i. 2.

Its effects are spoken of in the curse which Timon of Athens flings at the city which he has left :

> And yet confusion live !—Plagues, incident to men,
> Your potent and infectious fevers heap
> On Athens, ripe for stroke !   Thou cold sciatica,
> Cripple our senators, that their limbs may halt
> As lamely as their manners !   Lust and liberty
> Creep in the minds and marrows of our youth,
> That 'gainst the stream of virtue they may strive,

> And drown themselves in riot ! Itches, blains,
> Sow all the Athenian bosoms ; and their crop
> Be general leprosy ! Breath infect breath,
> That their society, as their friendship, may
> Be merely poison ! Nothing I'll bear from thee
> But nakedness, thou detestable town !
> *Timon of Athens*, iv. 1.

PALSY. The form of this affection, which is frequently referred to, is *Paralysis agitans* or the *Shaking palsy*, as when Lord Say, whom "long sitting to determine poor men's causes" had filled "with sickness and diseases," on being asked why he quivered, replied :

> It is the palsy, and not fear, provokes me.
> *II. Henry VI.* iv. 7.

It is associated with other defects of age in the passage in *Troilus and Cressida*, i. 3, quoted on p. 40.

HEMIPLEGIA is probably denoted in the following :

> O, then, how quickly should this arm of mine,
> Now prisoner to the palsy, chastise thee,
> And minister correction to thy fault ! *Richard II.* ii. 3.

APOPLEXY, with its lethargy and tingling, is mentioned below :

Peace is a very apoplexy, lethargy ; mulled, deaf, sleepy, insensible ; a getter of more bastard children than war's a destroyer of men. *Coriolanus*, iv. 5.

Fal. This apoplexy is, as I take it, a kind of lethargy, an't please your lordship : a kind of sleeping in the blood, a whoreson tingling.
II. Henry IV. i. 2.

CRAMPS ; CONVULSIONS ; PAIN IN THE SIDE ; BONE-ACHE.

> *Pro.* For this, be sure, to-night thou shalt have cramps,
> Side-stitches that shall pen thy breath up ; urchins
> Shall, for that vast of night that they may work,

All exercise on thee : thou shalt be pinch'd
As thick as honey-combs, each pinch more stinging
Than bees that made them. *Tempest*, i. 2.

Go, charge my goblins that they grind their joints
With dry convulsions ; shorten up their sinews
With aged cramps ; and more pinch-spotted make them
Than pard, or cat o' mountain. *Tempest*, iv. 1.

If thou neglect'st, or dost unwillingly
What I command, I'll rack thee with old cramps ;
Fill all thy bones with aches ; make thee roar,
That beasts shall tremble at thy din. *Tempest*, i. 2.

 In a retreat, he outruns any lackey ; marry, in coming on he has the cramp.   *All's Well that Ends Well*, iv. 3.

HYDROPHOBIA. This disease, though not mentioned by name, was known to Shakespeare. In the *Comedy of Errors* there is a passage where a fit of madness is ascribed to "The venom-clamours of a jealous woman," and this cause of madness is spoken of as a

 Poison more deadly than a mad dog's tooth.
  Comedy of Errors, v. 1.

The passage shows that he was aware of a mad dog's bite producing symptoms similar to those of a fit of insanity. But it is remarkable in other points as recognizing a connection between Melancholia and these three conditions, Insomnia, Dyspepsia, and the absence of due recreation.

 Abb. And thereof came it, that the man was mad:
The venom-clamours of a jealous woman
Poison more deadly than a mad dog's tooth.
It seems, his sleeps were hinder'd by thy railing :
And therefore comes it, that his head is light.
Thou say'st, his meat was sauced with thy upbraidings :
Unquiet meals make ill digestions,—
Thereof the raging fire of fever bred ;
And what's a fever but a fit of madness ?
Thou say'st his sports were hinder'd by thy brawls :

> Sweet recreation barr'd, what doth ensue,
> But moody and dull melancholy,
> Kinsman to grim and comfortless despair ;
> And, at her heels, a huge infectious troop
> Of pale distemperatures, and foes to life ?
> In food, in sport, and life-preserving rest
> To be disturb'd, would mad or man or beast :
> The consequence is, then, thy jealous fits
> Have scared thy husband from the use of wits.
>
> *Comedy of Errors*, v. 1.

Of the class of NERVOUS DISEASES, Epilepsy, Apoplexy, and Paralysis have already been taken notice of. In addition to these we have a case of *Catalepsy* in the trance during which the Queen in *Pericles* is thrown overboard and washed ashore in the "caulked and bitumed" chest. Skilful use of *Somnambulism* is made in the case of Lady Macbeth. *Visual Spectra,* from aberration of the subjective sensations, are seen by Macbeth on two occasions; one when he saw the dagger clotted with blood, and the other when he saw the figure of Banquo occupying the chair at the banquet.

The ghost in *Hamlet* may also be referred to in this connection, although the poet seems to intend its appearance as real, and Hamlet gives evidence from his pulse that the vision did not arise from any mental affection of his own (iii. 4).

The mere enumeration of these may suffice here, as they belong to the morbid Psychology of Shakespeare, which has been intentionally omitted, as stated in the preface.

HYSTERIA, then called "the mother," is spoken of by King Lear with evident allusion to the rising of the *Globus Hystericus.*

> *Lear.* O, how this mother swells up toward my heart !
> *Hysterica passio !*—down, thou climbing sorrow,
> Thy element's below !— *King Lear*, ii. 4.

Ecstasy seems to have been used in a very wide sense for varied states of mental disturbance and insanity. Thus Ophelia says of Hamlet :

> That unmatch'd form and feature of blown youth
> Blasted with ecstasy. *Hamlet*, iii. 1.

And again it occurs in Hamlet's discourse with his mother (iii. 4). In allusion to epilepsy we find it in *Othello*, iv. 1 (compare p. 29).

Sympathetic Disturbance, and the influence of the mind on the body, the influence of hope, despair, or apprehension, are all indicated in the following quotations :

> For let our finger ache, and it endues
> Our other healthful members ev'n to that sense
> Of pain. *Othello*, iii. 4.

> But where the greater malady is fix'd,
> The lesser is scarce felt. Thou'dst shun a bear :
> But if thy flight lay toward the raging sea,
> Thou'dst meet the bear i' the mouth. When the mind's free
> The body's delicate : the tempest in my mind
> Doth from my senses take all feeling else,
> Save what beats there. *King Lear*, iii. 4.

> *Macb.* The labour we delight in physics pain.
> *Macbeth*, ii. 3.

> *Claud.* The miserable have no other medicine,
> But only hope. *Measure for Measure*, iii. 1.

> *Rom.* Bid a sick man in sadness make his will :—
> Ah, word ill urged to one that is so ill !
> *Romeo and Juliet*, i. 1.

> Darest thou die?
> The sense of death is most in apprehension ;
> And the poor beetle, that we tread upon,
> In corporal sufferance finds a pang as great
> As when a giant dies. *Measure for Measure*, iii. 1.

In this same connection may be mentioned the temptation to throw oneself from a height by the mind contemplating the abyss:

think of it:
The very place puts toys of desperation,
Without more motive, into every brain,
That looks so many fathoms to the sea,
And hears it roar beneath. *Hamlet*, i. 4.

An allied passage in *King Lear* of *simulated* description may also be mentioned, beginning:

Edgar. Come on, sir, here's the place: stand still.—How fearful
And dizzy 'tis to cast one's eyes so low!
King Lear, iv. 6.

The influence of mental or emotional excitement on the circulation, and its tell-tale action from paleness or flushing, are referred to in the first quotation, and its effect on the vision in the second:

Bass. Madam, you have bereft me of all words,
Only my blood speaks to you in my veins.
Merchant of Venice, iii. 2.

Glo. Pardon me, gracious lord;
Some sudden qualm hath struck me at the heart,
And dimm'd mine eyes, that I can read no further.
II. Henry VI. i. 1.

COLIC. This ailment furnishes Hotspur with his mocking reply to Glendower; when Glendower boasts that at his birth the frame and huge foundation of the earth "shaked like a coward" Hotspur suggests that it has had a colic:

Hot. O, then, th' earth shook to see the heavens on fire,
And not in fear of your nativity.
Diseased nature oftentimes breaks forth
In strange eruptions: oft the teeming earth
Is with a kind of cholic pinch'd and vex'd

> By the imprisoning of unruly wind
> Within her womb; which, for enlargement striving,
> Shakes the old beldame earth, and topples down
> Steeples, and moss-grown towers. *I. Henry IV.* iii. 1.

That humorous patrician Menenius describes the conduct of the plebeians under the painful spasm of this ailment as follows:

> When you are hearing a matter between party and party, if you chance to be pinched with the cholic, you make faces like mummers; set up the bloody flag against all patience: and, in roaring for a chamber-pot, dismiss the controversy bleeding, the more entangled by your hearing: all the peace you make in their cause, is, calling both the parties knaves: You are a pair of strange ones.
> *Coriolanus,* ii. 1.

The tympanites in this ailment is alluded to by Ajax in this command:

> *Ajax.* Thou, trumpet, there's my purse.
> Now crack thy lungs, and split thy brazen pipe:
> Blow, villain, till thy sphered bias cheek
> Out-swell the colick of puff'd Aquilon:
> Come, stretch thy chest, and let thy eyes spout blood:
> Thou blow'st for Hector. *Troilus and Cressida,* iv. 5.

INTESTINAL WORMS are alluded to in a metaphorical sense, thus:

> Civil dissension is a viperous worm
> That gnaws the bowels of the commonwealth.
> *I. Henry VI.* iii. 1.

JAUNDICE. The only two references to this symptom are interesting from the fact that they recognize the connection between dull moods of the mind and affections of the liver. One of these is quoted above at page 13, "creep into the jaundice" (*Merchant of Venice,* i. 1). The other is:

> What grief hath set the jaundice on your cheeks?
> *Troilus and Cressida,* i. 3.

DISORDERS OF APPETITE AND DIGESTION. Some passages connected with digestion and indigestion may be classed together here, also loathing of food and perverted appetite.

> *Gaunt.* Things sweet to taste, prove in digestion sour.
> *Richard II.* i. 3.

> A sick man's appetite, who desires most that
> Which would increase his evil.   *Coriolanus*, i. 1.

> But, like in sickness, did I loathe this food:
> But, as in health, come to my natural taste,
> Now do I wish it, love it, long for it.
> *Midsummer-Night's Dream*, iv. i.

Cheese as an aid to digestion is here humorously referred to:

> *Achil.* Where, where?—Art thou come? Why, my cheese, my digestion, why hast thou not served thyself in to my table so many meals? Come, what's Agamemnon? *Troilus and Cressida*, ii. 3.

HEARTBURN is humorously referred to in this repartee in connection with Bardolph's red and burning face:

> *Bard.* 'Sblood, I would my face were in your belly!
> *Fal.* God-a-mercy! so should I be sure to be heart-burned.
> *I. Henry IV.* iii. 3.

The metaphorical allusion in the next is to the acidity which causes heartburn:

> *Beat.* How tartly that gentleman looks! I never can see him, but I am heart-burned an hour after.
> *Much Ado About Nothing*, ii. 1.

DROPSY. In a passage previously quoted (p. 15), Sir John Falstaff is spoken of contemptuously as a "parcel of dropsies" (*I. Henry IV.* ii. 4). The dropsical swelling is used metaphorically in *All's Well that Ends Well*, where the king says:

> From lowest place when virtuous things proceed,
> The place is dignified by the doer's deed:

> Where great additions swell, and virtue none,
> It is a dropsied honour.   *All's Well that Ends Well*, ii. 3.

In the *Tempest*, iv. 1, Caliban exclaims: "The dropsy drown this fool!" The phrase embodies what is at this day a popular belief as to how death takes place in dropsical cases, viz. that the water rises in the body until it drowns the heart.

GOUT is referred to in connection with advancing age, its liability to occur in the rich, and its tendency to recur.

> A man can no more separate age and covetousness, than he can part young limbs and lechery: but the gout galls the one, and the pox pinches the other; and so both the degrees prevent my curses.
> *II. Henry IV*. i. 2.

> *Ros.* With a priest that lacks Latin, and a rich man that hath not the gout, for the one sleeps easily because he cannot study, and the other lives merrily because he feels no pain; the one lacking the burden of lean and wasteful learning, the other knowing no burden of heavy tedious penury: these Time ambles withal.
> *As You Like It*, iii. 2.

> yet am I better
> Than one that's sick o' the gout; since he had rather
> Groan so in perpetuity, than be cured
> By the sure physician, death; who is the key
> To unbar these locks.   *Cymbeline*, v. 4.

The ambiguity of the diagnosis is admitted by Falstaff when he says:

> A pox of this gout! or, a gout of this pox! for the one or the other plays the rogue with my great toe.   *II. Henry IV*. i. 2.

PRURITUS, and its relief by scratching, are turned to good use, as where Caius Marcius in *Coriolanus*, coming upon the clamorous and discontented citizens, asks:

> What's the matter, you dissentious rogues,
> That rubbing the poor itch of your opinion,
> Make yourselves scabs?   *Coriolanus*, i. 1.

And in that most humorous passage-of-arms between Ajax and Thersites :

Ajax. Do not, porcupine, do not; my fingers itch.
Ther. I would thou didst itch from head to foot, and I had the scratching of thee; I would make thee the loathsomest scab in Greece.
Troilus and Cressida, ii. 1.

THE GREEN SICKNESS (*Chlorosis*) is referred to in *Romeo and Juliet*, but more as a term of abuse :

Out, you green-sickness Carrion ! out, you baggage !
You tallow-face !   *Romeo and Juliet*, iii. 5.

But men are also spoken of as having this disease :

and Lepidus,
Since Pompey's feast, as Menas says, is troubled
With the green sickness.   *Antony and Cleopatra*, iii. 2.

Falstaff also indicates this :

For thin drink doth so over-cool their blood, and making many fish meals, that they fall into a kind of male green sickness.
II. Henry IV. iv. 3.

In *Pericles* (iv. 5) the word also occurs, but apparently without reference to the disease known as such.

PULMONARY CONSUMPTION. Pandarus, in addition to the incurable boneache which we shall afterwards see to be syphilitic, had a wasting disease accompanied by a rheum, which, it is justifiable to assume, was pulmonary phthisis—although some may prefer to suppose this "ptisick" to be merely the wasting of chronic syphilis:

Pan. A whoreson ptisick, a whoreson rascally ptisick so troublesme, and the foolish fortune of this girl; and what one thing, what another, that I shall leave you one o' these days. And I have a rheum in mine eyes too ; and such an ache in my bones, that, unless a man were cursed, I cannot tell what to think on't—What says she there ?   *Troilus and Cressida*, v. 3.

The incurable nature of consumption gives occasion to Falstaff to say:

Fal. I can get no remedy against this consumption of the purse: borrowing only lingers and lingers it out, but the disease is incurable. *II. Henry IV.* i. 2.

Its pathology is graphically set down thus:

Adr. The air breathes upon us here most sweetly.
Seb. As if it had lungs, and rotten ones.
Tempest, ii. 1.

SENILE DECAY. There are perhaps few passages in the Plays more graphic than those in which a few master strokes suffice to set before us the symptoms of senile decay. The first is the familiar utterance of Jacques in *As You Like It*:

The sixth age shifts
Into the lean and slipper'd pantaloon;
With spectacles on nose, and pouch on side;
His youthful hose well saved, a world too wide
For his shrunk shank; and his big manly voice,
Turning again toward childish treble, pipes
And whistles in his sound. Last scene of all,
That ends this strange eventful history,
Is second childishness, and mere oblivion:
Sans teeth, sans eyes, sans taste, sans everything.
As You Like It, ii. 7.

Again:

Ch. Just. Do you set down your name in the scroll of youth, that are written down old with all the characters of age? Have you not a moist eye? a dry hand? a yellow cheek? a white beard? a decreasing leg? an increasing belly? Is not your voice broken? your wind short? your chin double? your wit single? and every part about you blasted with antiquity? and will you yet call yourself young? Fy, fy, fy, Sir John! *II. Henry IV.* i. 2.

Ham. Slanders, sir; for the satirical rogue says here, that old men have grey beards; that their faces are wrinkled; their eyes purging thick amber and plum-tree gum; and that they have a plentiful lack of wit, together with most weak hams.
Hamlet, ii. 2.

> And then, forsooth, the faint defects of age
> Must be the scene of mirth : to cough and spit,
> And with a palsy-fumbling on his gorget,
> Shake in and out the rivet. *Troilus and Cressida*, i. 3.

IN ARTICULO MORTIS. Besides the deaths of Falstaff and King John already mentioned (pp. 24 and 25), there are three others worthy of study, viz. those of Mortimer in *I. Henry VI.*, Queen Catherine in *Henry VIII.*, and Cardinal Beaufort in *II. Henry VI.* The following quotations from the two former are of interest, the one for the poetic beauty no less than the truth of the description, and the other as noting the change which comes over the countenance presaging dissolution :

> *Mor.* Kind keepers of my weak decaying age,
> Let dying Mortimer here rest himself.
> Even like a man new haled from the rack,
> So fare my limbs with long imprisonment :
> And these grey locks, the pursuivants of death,
> Nestor-like aged, in an age of care,
> Argue the end of Edmund Mortimer.
> These eyes,—like lamps whose wasting oil is spent,—
> Wax dim, as drawing to their exigent :
> Weak shoulders, overborne with burd'ning grief :
> And pithless arms, like to a wither'd vine
> That droops his sapless branches to the ground :
> Yet are these feet—whose strengthless stay is numb,
> Unable to support this lump of clay,—
> Swift-wingèd with desire to get a grave,
> As witting I no other comfort have. *I. Henry VI.* ii. 5.

> *Pat.* Do you note,
> How much her grace is alter'd on the sudden ?
> How long her face is drawn ? How pale she looks
> And of an earthly cold ? Mark you her eyes ?
> *Grif.* She is going, wench ; pray, pray.
> *Pat.* Heaven comfort her ! *Henry VIII.* iv. 2.

The death scene of the Cardinal is complicated by the

utterances of despair and remorse associated with visions of past crimes:

> *K. Hen.* How fares my lord? Speak, Beaufort, to thy sovereign.
> *Card.* If thou be'st Death, I'll give thee England's treasure,
> Enough to purchase such another island,
> So thou wilt let me live, and feel no pain.
> *K. Hen.* Ah, what a sign it is of evil life,
> Where death's approach is seen so terrible!
> *War.* Beaufort, it is thy sovereign speaks to thee.
> *Card.* Bring me unto my trial when you will.
> Died he not in his bed? Where should he die?
> Can I make men live, whe'r they will or no?
> O, torture me no more! I will confess.—
> Alive again? Then show me where he is:
> I'll give a thousand pound to look upon him.
> He hath no eyes, the dust hath blinded them.
> Comb down his hair; look, look! it stands upright,
> Like lime-twigs set to catch my winged soul!
> Give me some drink; and bid th' apothecary
> Bring the strong poison that I bought of him.
> *K. Hen.* O thou eternal Mover of the heavens,
> Look with a gentle eye upon this wretch!
> O, beat away the busy-meddling fiend
> That lays strong siege unto this wretch's soul,
> And from his bosom purge this black despair!
> *War.* See how the pangs of death do make him grin!
> *Sal.* Disturb him not: let him pass peaceably.
> *K. Hen.* Peace to his soul, if God's good pleasure be!
> Lord Cardinal, if thou think'st on heaven's bliss,
> Hold up thy hand, make signal of thy hope,—
> He dies, and makes no sign:—O God forgive him!
>
> *II. Henry VI.* iii. 3.

(See also the deaths of Falstaff and King John referred to at pp. 24, 25.)

POST-MORTEM APPEARANCES. A very remarkable comparison is instituted between death from natural causes and that from violence, in the speech of Warwick as he and the others stand by the bedside of the murdered Gloster. The signs are those of death by strangulation after a struggle:

> *War.* See how the blood is settled in his face.
> Oft have I seen a timely-parted ghost,
> Of ashy semblance, meagre, pale, and bloodless,
> Being all descended to the labouring heart;
> Who, in the conflict that it holds with death,
> Attracts the same for aidance 'gainst the enemy;
> Which with the heart there cools, and ne'er returneth
> To blush and beautify the cheek again.
> But, see, his face is black, and full of blood;
> His eye-balls further out than when he lived,
> Staring full ghastly like a strangled man:
> His hair uprear'd, his nostrils stretch'd with struggling:
> His hands abroad display'd, as one that grasp'd
> And tugg'd for life, and was by strength subdued.
> Look, on the sheets his hair, you see, is sticking;
> His well-proportion'd beard made rough and rugged,
> Like to the summer's corn by tempest lodg'd.
> It cannot be but he was murder'd here:
> The least of all these signs were probable.
> *II. Henry VI.* iii. 2.

The swollen appearance of the body in death by drowning is spoken of by Falstaff:

> I had been drowned, but that the shore was shelvy and shallow, a death that I abhor; for the water swells a man; and what a thing should I have been, when I had been swelled! I should have been a mountain of mummy. *Merry Wives of Windsor*, iii. 5.

DIAGNOSIS. The three modes of clinical diagnosis which we find in Shakespeare, keeping out of view at present external appearances, are the character of the pulse, the examination of the urine, and changes in the expectoration.

THE PULSE. The increased rapidity of the pulse in fever has been spoken of already (p. 23). In the *Comedy of Errors*, Pinch, the conjurer, is spoken of as "feeling my pulse" (v. 1.), and in another passage he is represented as saying:

> Give me your hand, and let me feel your pulse.
> *Comedy of Errors*, iv. 4.

In *Hamlet*, where the Queen sets down Hamlet's vision of the ghost, as "the very coinage of your brain," etc., Hamlet replies:

> *Ham.* Ecstasy!
> My pulse, as yours, doth temperately keep time,
> And makes as healthful music: It is not madness
> That I have utter'd: bring me to the test
> And I the matter will re-word, which madness
> Would gambol from. *Hamlet*, iii. 4.

In these cases the pulse is appealed to, in order to decide between sanity and insanity.

In some other references the pulse may be regarded rather as physiological than as diagnostic of diseased states. Thus the Hostess of the Boar's Head says to Doll Tearsheet:

> Your pulsidge beats as extraordinarily as heart would desire.
> *II. Henry IV.* ii. 4.

King John asks:

> Have I commandment on the pulse of life?
> *King John*, iv. 2.

Alonzo makes sure of Prospero's reality as a man when he says:

> thy pulse
> Beats, as of flesh and blood. *Tempest*, v. 1.

In a similar sense Pericles asks:

> But are you flesh and blood?
> Have you a working pulse? and are no fairy?
> *Pericles*, v. 1.

EXAMINATION OF URINE. The diagnosis of disease from the naked-eye appearances of the urine was so diligently cultivated about Shakespeare's time, that it had risen to the dignity of a specialty. A class existed who professed only this branch of the art, and amusing anecdotes are told of their successes and failures in diagnosis. The practice is taken notice of in four different Plays. It is applied metaphorically by Macbeth, when a forecast from the urine is desired in making out the cause of his country's disorder :

> If thou couldst, doctor, cast
> The water of my land, find her disease,
> And purge it to a sound and pristine health,
> I would applaud thee to the very echo,
> That should applaud again.—Pull't off, I say.—
> What rhubarb, senna, or what purgative drug,
> Would scour these English hence? *Macbeth*, v. 3.

And also by Speed, in the passage :

Speed. Without you; nay, that's certain, for, without you were so simple, none else would : but you are so without these follies, that these follies are within you, and shine through you like the water in an urinal;[1] that not an eye, that sees you, but is a physician to comment on your malady. *Two Gentlemen of Verona*, ii. 1.

In the question as to whether Malvolio was bewitched, Fabian suggests that his urine be examined :

Mar. La you, an you speak ill of the devil, how he takes it at heart ! Pray God, he be not bewitched !
Fab. Carry his water to the wise woman.
Mar. Marry, and it shall be done to-morrow morning, if I live. My lady would not lose him for more than I'll say.
Twelfth Night, iii. 4.

Falstaff, besides having ague, is lame from an affection

---

[1] A glass vessel used for inspecting urine in diagnosis.

of his great toe, of which he doubts as to its being gouty or syphilitic in its origin:

Fal. A pox of this gout! or a gout of this pox! for the one or the other plays the rogue with my great toe. It is no matter, if I do halt; I have the wars for my colour, and my pension shall seem the more reasonable. A good wit will make use of anything; I will turn diseases to commodity. *II. Henry IV.* i. 2.

We do not wonder therefore at his sending a sample of his water to the doctor, or that the latter should send back such an oracular reply:

Fal. Sirrah, you giant, what says the doctor to my water?
Page. He said, sir, the water itself was a good healthy water; but, for the party that owed it, he might have more diseases than he knew for. *II. Henry IV.* i. 2.

EXPECTORATION. The importance of this is recognized by Falstaff in his imprecation:

If it be a hot day, and I brandish anything but my bottle, I would I might never spit white again. *II. Henry IV.* i. 2.

Some commentators have supposed that "spitting white" resulted from indulgence in drinking, and that this is the allusion. The more natural meaning here seems to be the contrast between "spitting white" and "spitting yellow," the latter being so common in bad cases of bronchitis and consumption, as compared with a simple whitish spittle. Compare also *Troilus and Cressida*, i. 3, quoted at p. 40.

Note.—References to Insanity are purposely excluded from this Thesis; for these consult the Bibliography. Venereal diseases are dealt with in a section under SURGERY.

CHAPTER III

MATERIA MEDICA, TOXICOLOGY, AND THERAPEUTICS

BEFORE speaking of "medicine" as an article administered in the cure of disease, it may be well to recall the use of this word by Shakespeare in the sense of a physician (French *médecin*). Thus, in *Macbeth*, we find:

>*Caith.* Well, march we on,
>To give obedience where 'tis truly ow'd:
>Meet we the medicine of the sickly weal,
>And with him pour we in our country's purge
>Each drop of us.   *Macbeth*, v. 2.

In the following passage the word "medicine" is used in the same way, but in this instance refers to a "lady doctor":

>I have seen a medicine
>That's able to breathe life into a stone,
>Quicken a rock, and make you dance canary
>With sprightly fire and motion; whose simple touch
>Is powerful to araise king Pepin, nay,
>To give great Charlemain a pen in his hand
>And write to her a love-line.
>*King.*   What "her" is this?
>*Laf.* Why, doctor She, etc.
>   *All's Well that Ends Well*, ii. 1.

Again,
>Preserver of my father, now of me,
>The medicine of our house!   *Winter's Tale*, iv. 3.

MATERIA MEDICA, TOXICOLOGY, THERAPEUTICS

The preparations and modes of administering medicines spoken of in the plays are oils, balsams, syrups, infusions,[1] plasters, poultices, cataplasms, salves, potions, and pills, sleepy drinks, caudles,[2] and clysters.

The names of medicinal agents mentioned are ACONITUM; AQUA VITAE; CIVET; COLOQUINTIDA; HEBENON; MANDRAGORA; MUSK; PARMACETI; POPPY; RATSBANE; RHUBARB; SENNA[3]; SUGAR CANDY; WINE.

NARCOTICS. Many of the medicines named above receive a mere passing mention, and we shall consider those first which influence the action of the plays. These are, as might be expected, the poisons and narcotics. In the play of *Cymbeline*, the queen is represented as having studied, under the guidance of Cornelius, the physician, such acts of pharmacy as the making of perfumes, distilling, and preserving, but she does so for the purpose of procuring poisons with which to carry out her wicked designs. In the fifth scene of the first act, she enquires of Cornelius if he has brought the drugs, and he, presenting her with the box, asks in return:

> Wherefore you have
> Commanded of me these most poisonous compounds,
> Which are the movers of a languishing death;
> But, though slow, deadly?   *Cymbeline*, i. 5.

We quote the rest of the conversation as an early but

---

[1] The blest infusions
That dwell in vegetives.   *Pericles*, iii. 2.

This seems to refer to the active substances *in* plants rather than to pharmaceutical infusions made *from* them. The phrase "Hot infusion" (*Winter's Tale*, iv. 3) seems to refer to brandy and water (see p. 60).

[2] "A Caudle, ho!" (*Love's Labour's Lost*, iv. 3).

[3] See p. 62.

able anticipation of the vivisection controversy, and one in which the laity and the profession occupy positions to some extent the reverse of those of to-day:

> *Queen.* I do wonder, doctor,
> Thou ask'st me such a question: Have I not been
> Thy pupil long? Hast thou not learn'd me how
> To make perfumes? distil? preserve? yea, so
> That our great king himself doth woo me oft
> For my confections? Having thus far proceeded,
> (Unless thou think'st me devilish,) is't not meet
> That I did amplify my judgment in
> Other conclusions? I will try the forces
> Of these thy compounds on such creatures as
> We count not worth the hanging (but none human),
> To try the vigour of them, and apply
> Allayments to their act; and by them gather
> Their several virtues and effects.
>   *Cor.* Your highness
> Shall from this practice but make hard your heart:
> Besides, the seeing these effects will be
> Both noisome and infectious.   *Cymbeline,* i. 5.

Dr. Cornelius practises the pardonable deception of giving her, not the poison she expects, but an innocent narcotic:

> *Cor. (Aside).* I do not like her. She doth think she has
> Strange lingering poisons: I do know her spirit,
> And will not trust one of her malice with
> A drug of such damn'd nature. Those she has
> Will stupify and dull the sense awhile;
> Which first, perchance, she'll prove on cats and dogs,
> Then afterward up higher; but there is
> No danger in what show of death it makes,
> More than the locking up the spirits a time,
> To be more fresh, reviving. She is fool'd
> With a most false effect; and I the truer,
> So to be false with her.   *Cymbeline,* i. 5.

In the development of the play the box comes to Imogen with the recommendation

> Here is a box ; I had it from the queen :
> What's in't is precious ; if you are sick at sea,
> Or stomach-qualm'd at land, a dram of this
> Will drive away distemper.   *Cymbeline*, iii. 4.

She tastes of the drug in the cave of Belarius, and the slumber ensuing lasts, to judge from the action of the play, several hours. When discovered she is supposed to be dead and to have died of melancholy. "How found you him," asks Belarius, and is answered :

> *Arv.* Stark, as you see :
> Thus smiling, as some fly had tickled slumber,
> Not as death's dart, being laugh'd at : his right cheek
> Reposing on a cushion.   *Cymbeline*, iv. 2.

On awaking she does not at first remember what has taken place, but imagines she is still walking towards Milford Haven. The effect of the drug does not pass off at once, for she is about to yield again to slumber, when she discovers the headless body of Cloten in the dress of Posthumus.

The similarity between the action of this drug and that which the Friar gives to Juliet will at once strike the reader, as well as the similarity of the circumstances in which each finds herself on awaking : both are beside the dead bodies of their lovers, Imogen in her cave, and Juliet in the tomb. But in *Romeo and Juliet* the action of the drug is more fully detailed by the Friar :

> Take thou this phial, being then in bed,
> And this distilled liquor drink thou off :
> When presently through all thy veins shall run
> A cold and drowsy humour, which shall seize
> Each vital spirit ; for no pulse shall keep
> His natural progress, but surcease to beat :
> No warmth, no breath, shall testify thou livest ;
> The roses in thy lips and cheeks shall fade
> To paly ashes ; thy eyes' windows fall,

> Like death, when he shuts up the day of life ;
> Each part, deprived of supple government,
> Shall, stiff and stark and cold, appear like death :
> And in this borrow'd likeness of shrunk death
> Thou shalt remain full two and forty hours,
> And then awake as from a pleasant sleep.
>
> *Romeo and Juliet*, iv. 1.

The Friar's statement that the "roses in thy cheeks and lips shall fade to paly ashes," would seem inconsistent with Romeo's soliloquy:

> Beauty's ensign yet
> Is crimson in thy lips, and in thy cheeks,
> And death's pale flag is not advanced there.
>
> *Romeo and Juliet*, v. 3.

but when he spoke thus, she was near the point of awaking.

It is impossible on these data to say that Shakespeare had the action of any particular narcotic in mind, although there are points in the Friar's description which favour the idea of some preparation of opium. These are the slowness of the pulse, the retarded respiration, the pallor of the lips and cheeks, the ghastly deathlike appearance, and the awaking after a long interval as from a pleasant sleep. The description is so truthful that Shakespeare must have been familiar with some of the appearances and effects of narcotism; but, on the other hand, had he been fully conversant with the properties of opium, he would hardly have described the Friar as embarking on the dangerous experiment of giving a quantity sufficient to produce forty-two hours' consecutive slumber, and as being able to predict to an hour the cessation of its action. That he knew of more than one narcotic, we learn from the beautiful passage which he puts into the mouth of the physician in *King Lear*.

> *Phy.* There is means, madam :
> Our foster-nurse of nature is repose,

> The which he lacks ; that to provoke in him,
> Are many simples operative, whose power
> Will close the eye of anguish. *King Lear*, iv. 4.

The other passages alluding to narcotics are, where Archidamus in *Winter's Tale* says :

> We will give you sleepy drinks, that your senses, unintelligent of our insufficience, may, though they cannot praise us, as little accuse us. *Winter's Tale*, i. 1.

where Lady Macbeth drugs the possets of the grooms on the night of the murder:

> I have drugged their possets,
> That death and nature do contend about them,
> Whether they live or die. *Macbeth*, ii. 1.

where Iago says of Othello :

> Look where he comes ! Not poppy, nor mandragora,
> Nor all the drowsy syrups of the world,
> Shall ever medicine thee to that sweet sleep
> Which thou ow'dst yesterday. *Othello*, iii. 3.

and where Cleopatra, calling for mandragora (mandrake), says :

> *Cleo.* Ha, ha !
> Give me to drink mandragora.
> *Char.* Why, madam ?
> *Cleo.* That I might sleep out this great gap of time,
> My Antony is away. *Antony and Cleopatra*, i. 5.

OTHER POISONS are mentioned in a great many different connections. Distinctions are drawn between their medicinal effect given in small doses and their poisonous effect in large. The most noteworthy example of these is the well-known passage in *Romeo and Juliet*, where Friar Laurence says :

> O, mickle is the powerful grace that lies
> In herbs, plants, stones, and their true qualities :
> For nought so vile that on the earth doth live

> But to the earth some special good doth give;
> Nor aught so good but strain'd from that fair use,
> Revolts from true birth, stumbling on abuse:
> Virtue itself turns vice, being misapplied;
> And vice sometime's by action dignified.
> Within the infant rind of this small flower
> Poison hath residence and med'cine power:
> For this, being smelt, with that part cheers each part;
> Being tasted, slays all senses with the heart.
> Two such opposed foes encamp them still
> In man as well as herbs, grace and rude will;
> And where the worser is predominant,
> Full soon the canker death eats up that plant.
> *Romeo and Juliet*, ii. 3.

The different action of a poison in health and in disease is noticed. Northumberland says:

> In poison there is physic; and these news,
> Having been well, that would have made me sick,
> Being sick, have in some measure made me well.
> *II. Henry IV*. i. 1.

The different action of the same agent in different states, or different doses, is well shown by Lady Macbeth:

> That which hath made them drunk hath made me bold;
> What hath quench'd them hath given me fire.
> *Macbeth*, ii. 2.

Among the poisons mentioned by name, we find aconitum (wolfsbane or monkshood). King Henry closes his admonition to Clarence as to how to deal with the Prince in these words:

> And thou shalt prove a shelter to thy friends,
> A hoop of gold to bind thy brothers in,
> That the united vessel of their blood,
> Mingled with venom of suggestion
> (As, force perforce, the age will pour it in)
> Shall never leak, though it do work as strong
> As aconitum or rash gunpowder.
> *II. Henry IV*. iv. 4.

Sir John Falstaff, in the same play, where Dombledon the draper requires security before giving him the satin, speaks of ratsbane:

> I had as lief they would put ratsbane in my mouth as offer to stop it with security.
> *II. Henry IV.* i. 2.

This ratsbane occurs again in connection with an evil wish:

> Now cursed be the time
> Of thy nativity! I would the milk
> Thy mother gave thee when thou suck'dst her breast,
> Had been a little ratsbane for thy sake!
> *I. Henry VI.* v. 4.

Again, Edgar in his simulation of madness says:

> Set ratsbane by his porridge.
> *King Lear*, iii. 4.

Arsenic (arsenious acid) was probably indicated by this term ratsbane, and although not mentioned by name, arsenic would seem to be indicated in some passages.

One is in *Cymbeline*, where the Doctor says:

> *Cor.* More, sir, and worse. She did confess she had
> For you a mortal mineral, which, being took,
> Should by the minute feed on life, and ling'ring
> By inches waste you: in which time she purposed,
> By watching, weeping, tendance, kissing, to
> O'ercome you with her show: yes, and in time,
> (When she had fitted you with her craft,) to work
> Her son into the adoption of the crown.
> *Cymbeline*, v. 5.

This description is quite consistent with chronic poisoning by arsenic. Even more directly pointing to it is the metaphor used by Iago:

> Dangerous conceits are, in their natures, poisons,
> Which at the first are scarce found to distaste,
> But with a little act upon the blood
> Burn like the mines of sulphur.
> *Othello*, iii. 3.

There is also some internal evidence to show that arsenic was the poison administered to King John. The monk who poisoned him acted the part of taster and died immediately as here narrated:

> *Hub.* The king, I fear, is poisoned by a monk:
> I left him almost speechless, and broke out
> To acquaint you with this evil, that you might
> The better arm you to the sudden time,
> Than if you had at leisure known of this.
> *Bast.* How did he take it? who did taste to him?
> *Hub.* A monk, I tell you; a resolved villain,
> Whose bowels suddenly burst out: the king
> Yet speaks, and peradventure may recover.
> *King John,* v. 6.

"The bowels suddenly burst out" is not an unlikely popular description of the severe diarrhoea, which is a frequent symptom of arsenical poisoning, especially as this is often accompanied by discharges of blood, and in some cases of a material closely resembling green paint. (See Guy's *Forensic Medicine,* p. 447.) The delirium of the king already discussed is a rarer symptom though one not unknown, occurring in three out of twenty-five cases analyzed by Dr. Guy. The extreme debility, the thirst, the burning of the mouth and throat symptomatic of arsenical poisoning find their adequate literary expression in these lines:

> There is so hot a summer in my bosom,
> That all my bowels crumble up to dust:
> I am a scribbled form, drawn with a pen
> Upon a parchment, and against this fire
> Do I shrink up.
> *P. Hen.* How fares your majesty?
> *K. John.* Poison'd,—ill fare;—dead, forsook, cast off:
> And none of you will bid the winter come,
> To thrust his icy fingers in my maw;
> Nor let my kingdom's rivers take their course

> Through my burn'd bosom ; nor entreat the north
> To make his bleak winds kiss my parched lips
> And comfort me with cold. I do not ask you much,
> I beg cold comfort : and you are so strait
> And so ingrateful, you deny me that.
>   P. Hen. O that there were some virtue in my tears,
> That might relieve you !
>   K. John. The salt in them is hot.
> Within me is a hell : and there the poison
> Is as a fiend confined to tyrannize
> An unreprievable condemned blood.   *King John*, v. 7.

The poison which Romeo bought of the apothecary suggests from the swiftness of its action hydrocyanic acid, which however had not then been isolated as such :

> Ap. Who calls so loud ?
> Rom. Come hither, man. I see that thou art poor ;
> Hold, there is forty ducats : let me have
> A dram of poison, such soon-speeding gear
> As will disperse itself through all the veins
> That the life-weary taker may fall dead,
> And that the trunk may be discharged of breath
> As violently as hasty powder fired
> Doth hurry from the fatal cannon's womb.
>   *Romeo and Juliet*, v. 1.

In Hamlet three poisons are called into play. The one with which Laertes envenoms his sword that he may slay Hamlet appears to have been a powerful extract for whose effect there was no antidote. Laertes says of it :

> I bought an unction of a mountebank,
> So mortal that, but dip a knife in it,
> Where it draws blood, no cataplasm so rare,
> Collected from all simples that have virtue
> Under the moon, can save the thing from death
> That is but scratch'd withal : I'll touch my point
> With this contagion, that if I gall him slightly,
> It may be death.   *Hamlet*, iv. 7.

This is an instance of poisoning by inoculation like the arrow poisons used by savages, and the description of its deadly effect accords with the action of Curare. Of the poison prepared by the king lest Hamlet should escape Laertes' sword, we know nothing but that its action was instantaneous.

Of more interest than either of these is the "juice of cursed hebenon," with which Hamlet's father was poisoned. The Ghost relates the occurrence as follows:

>   Sleeping within mine orchard,
> My custom always of the afternoon,
> Upon my secure hour thy uncle stole
> With juice of cursed hebenon in a vial,
> And in the porches of mine ears did pour
> The leperous distilment ; whose effect
> Holds such an enmity with blood of man
> That, swift as quicksilver, it courses through
> The natural gates and alleys of the body,
> And, with a sudden vigour, it doth posset
> And curd, like eager droppings into milk,
> The thin and wholesome blood : so did it mine ;
> And a most instant tetter bark'd about,
> Most lazar-like, with vile and loathsome crust,
> All my smooth body.   *Hamlet*, i. 5.

The usual explanation of hebenon (Hebona in the Quarto) is to regard it as a transliteration of Henbane (or Hyoscyamus), which was referred to by Shakespeare as "the insane root" (radix insana) in *Macbeth*, i. 3. But there are grave objections to this interpretation, which are set forth at great length by Dr. Brinsley Nicholson in a paper on "Hamlet's Cursed Hebenon," in the *Transactions of the New Shakespeare Society*, Nov. 14, 1879 (*Transactions*, 1880-86, p. 21). His views are essentially confirmed in another elaborate paper in the same *Transactions* (May 12, 1882, p. 295) by the Rev. W. A. Harrison. Both writers agree in ascribing the poison to the yew, and they give contemporary evidence on the subject of this poison, with even quite modern confirmations as to its action agreeing with Shakespeare's description. To these papers the reader is referred for an elaborate discussion of this interesting subject. The same view is taken in Grindon's *Flora of Shakespeare*. The author states that he had taught this for many years before the appearance of the papers referred to. Without going into details regarding the etymology of the word, the following line from Spenser's *Faerie Queen* (Book I., Introduction iii.) may be quoted as showing the current use of the word:

> Lay now thy deadly heben bowe apart.

The passage in *Richard II.* (iii. 2) indicates that Shakespeare regarded the yew as "doubly fatal"—poisonous, as well as deadly from the weapons obtained from it:

> to bend their Bowes
> Of double fatall Eugh.

Other suppositions make hebenon equivalent to hemlock, and in the New Sydenham Society's *Lexicon* it is stated that "some suppose the juice of cursed hebenon of Shakespeare is the crude oil of tobacco, *Nicotiana tabacum*."

An undoubted allusion to Henbane (*Hyoscyamus: Insana radix*) refers especially to the visual spectra and the disturbance of the nervous system often produced in those who partake of it. Banquo asks:

> *Ban.* Were such things here as we do speak about?
> Or have we eaten of the insane root
> That takes the reason prisoner?   *Macbeth*, i. 3.

It is worthy of note that this is the only passage in Shakespeare where the word "insane" occurs: "insanie" occurs only once also (*Love's Labour's Lost*, v. 1).

The two following quotations infer the existence of

some poison which only manifested its effects a considerable time after being taken. This merely shows, what has appeared already in the discussion of the subject, that in old times there were highly imaginary poisons which had no counterpart in nature:

> *Cam.* Sir, my lord,
> I could do this; and that with no rash potion,
> But with a ling'ring dram that should not work
> Maliciously like poison. *Winter's Tale*, i. 2.

> *Gon.* All three of them are desperate; their great guilt,
> Like poison given to work a great time after,
> Now 'gins to bite the spirits. *Tempest*, iii. 3.

The following evidently embodies a popular belief, though what has given rise to it is not clear:

> *Ces.* O noble weakness!
> If they had swallow'd poison, 'twould appear
> By external swelling: but she looks like sleep,
> As she would catch another Antony
> In her strong toil of grace. *Antony and Cleopatra*, v. 2.

Alcoholic Liquors. It will not be necessary to dwell long on these, as it is a singular fact that although wine, beer, and ale receive frequent mention, they are hardly ever alluded to as medicinal agents. Wine, it is true, is often coupled with feeding, but in the large majority of cases the drinking of wine is introduced as a social custom, or as taken with the distinct purpose of producing intoxication. One exception to this appears in a passage already quoted (*Tempest*, ii. 2), where Stephano gives wine to Caliban to cure him of his ague, and another, where Antony dying, calls for it as a restorative:

> *Ant.* I am dying, Egypt, dying:
> Give me some wine, and let me speak a little.
> *Antony and Cleopatra*, iv. 13.

The effects of wine upon the liver have already been spoken of (p. 12), and its physiological effects on the brain when taken in moderation are described by Falstaff in the same passage:

> But that's no marvel, he drinks no wine. There's never any of these demure boys come to any proof: for thin drink doth so over-cool their blood, and making many fish-meals, that they fall into a kind of male green-sickness; and then, when they marry, they get wenches; they are generally fools and cowards,—which some of us should be too, but for inflammation. A good sherris-sack hath a two-fold operation in it. It ascends me into the brain; dries me there all the foolish, and dull, and crudy vapours, which environ it; makes it apprehensive, quick, forgetive, full of nimble, fiery, and delectable shapes: which, deliver'd o'er to the voice, (the tongue,) which is the birth, becomes excellent wit.
> *II. Henry IV.* iv. 3.

The following passage from *Macbeth* is a somewhat forcible description of the effects of alcohol when taken to excess:

> *Macd.* Was it so late, friend, ere you went to bed, that you do lie so late?
> *Port.* 'Faith, sir, we were carousing till the second cock: and drink, sir, is a great provoker of three things.
> *Macd.* What three things does drink especially provoke?
> *Port.* Marry, sir, nose-painting, sleep, and urine. Lechery, sir, it provokes, and unprovokes; it provokes the desire, but it takes away the performance. Therefore, much drink may be said to be an equivocator with lechery: it makes him, and it mars him; it sets him on, and it takes him off; it persuades him, and disheartens him; makes him stand to, and not stand to; in conclusion, equivocates him in a sleep, and, giving him the lie, leaves him.
> *Macbeth*, ii. 3.

Aqua vitæ—the designation applied to any distilled spirit of an intoxicating nature is grouped, in the *Comedy of Errors* (iv. 1), with the oil and balsamum which Dromio of Syracuse bought for the homeward voyage. It is mentioned in several places, and as a remedial agent it occurs in *Winter's Tale*, where its association with the phrase "hot infusion" is to be specially noted:

Aut. He has a son, who shall be flayed alive; then 'nointed over with honey, set on the head of a wasp's nest; then stand till he be three-quarters and a dram dead; then recovered again with aqua-vitæ or some other hot infusion. *Winter's Tale*, iv. 3.

As a beverage it seems to have been as well known to the midwives of that time as to the contemporaries of Sarah Gamp:

Mar. Nay, but say true; does it work upon him?
Sir To. Like aqua-vitæ with a midwife.
Twelfth Night, ii. 5.

Aphrodisiacs. Brabantio accuses Othello of having unlawfully made use of these to win over Desdemona:

Judge me the world, if 'tis not gross in sense
That thou hast practised on her with foul charms,
Abused her delicate youth with drugs or minerals
That weaken motion : I'll have it disputed on ;
'Tis probable, and palpable to thinking.
I therefore apprehend and do attach thee
For an abuser of the world, a practiser
Of arts inhibited and out of warrant. *Othello*, i. 2.

Again, we have the same idea in another play:

If the rascal have not given me medicines to make me love him, I'll be hanged; it could not be else : I have drunk medicines.— Poins! Hal! a plague upon you both! *I. Henry IV.* ii. 2.

The eryngo and potato seem to have been credited with properties of this kind:

Let the sky rain potatoes; let it thunder to the tune of *Green sleeves*, hail kissing-comfits and snow eryngoes; let there come a tempest of provocation, I will shelter me here.
Merry Wives of Windsor, v. 5.

The phrase in *Troilus and Cressida* (v. 2) "potato-finger" has a similar allusion.

See also under *Alcoholic Liquors* (p. 59).

Oils, Balsams. The following passages may be quoted under this heading:

> Pierced to the soul with slander's venom'd spear,
> The which no balm can cure, but his heart-blood
> Which breathed this poison. *Richard II.* i. 1.

> As true thou tell'st me, when I say I love her;
> But, saying thus, instead of oil and balm,
> Thou lay'st in every gash that love hath given me
> The knife that made it. *Troilus and Cressida,* i. 1.

> Is this the balsam that the usuring senate
> Pours into captains' wounds? ha! banishment!
> *Timon of Athens,* iii. 5.

> *Com.* Though I could wish
> You were conducted to a gentle bath
> And balms applied to you. *Coriolanus,* i. 6.

> My pity hath been balm to heal their wounds.
> *III. Henry VI.* iv. 8.

Syrups.

> *Abb.* Be patient: for I will not let him stir
> Till I have used the approved means I have,
> With wholesome syrups, drugs, and holy prayers,
> To make of him a formal man again.
> *Comedy of Errors,* v. 1.

Gums. The sources from which these are obtained furnish the beautiful image

> Of one whose subdued eyes,
> Albeit unused to the melting mood,
> Drop tears as fast as the Arabian trees
> Their medicinal gum. *Othello,* v. 2.

Rhubarb and *Senna* with their powerful action as purgatives are spoken of by Macbeth in connection with scouring the English out of his country :

> What rhubarb, senna, or what purgative drug,
> Would scour these English hence? *Macbeth*, v. 3.

Some doubt, however, has been expressed as to whether senna is really meant. The Folio has "Cyme," which has been supposed to be a natural misprint for "Cynne" (senna). (See Murray's *English Dictionary*, CYME.) Some, however, would read "Clysme" instead.

Parmaceti evidently means spermaceti :

> And telling me, the sovereign'st thing on earth
> Was parmaceti for an inward bruise.
> *I. Henry IV.* i. 3.

Coloquintida, the fruit of the Citrullus colocynthis, the cathartic medicine known as colocynth, is made use of in *Othello*, where Iago says :

Fill thy purse with money: the food that to him now is as luscious as locusts, shall be to him shortly as bitter as coloquintida. *Othello*, i. 3.

Civet. This perfume is spoken of several times. King Lear, at the close of that unsavoury passage beginning "Ay, every inch a King," calls out for a perfume :

Fy, fy, fy! pah, pah! Give me an ounce of civet, good apothecary, to sweeten my imagination : there's money for thee.
King Lear, iv. 6.

In *Much Ado About Nothing* (iii. 2.), Don Pedro says that Benedict rubs himself with civet and asks, "Can you smell him out by that?"

Touchstone with bantering philosophy proves to Corin that a shepherd's hands are cleaner than a courtier's; the source of the perfume is there mentioned.

Touch. Most shallow man! Thou worms-meat, in respect of a good piece of flesh, indeed! Learn of the wise, and perpend: Civet is of a baser birth than tar; the very uncleanly flux of a cat. Mend the instance, shepherd.   *As You Like It*, iii. 2.

Yew. This is referred to under "Cursed hebenon" (see page 56).

Camomile is mentioned once by Falstaff, as a plant growing the better the more it is trodden on, but it is not referred to as a medicine (*I. Henry IV.* ii. 4).

PHARMACEUTICAL PREPARATIONS. The following are the modes of administering medicines:

Potions.

  Lys. Thy love? out, tawny Tartar, out!
  Out, loathed medicine! hated potion, hence!
      Midsummer-Night's Dream, iii. 2.

Am I politic? am I subtle? am I a Machiavel? Shall I lose my doctor? no, he gives me the potions and the motions.
      Merry Wives of Windsor, iii. 1.

  For that same word, rebellion, did divide
  The action of their bodies from their souls;
  And they did fight with queasiness, constrain'd,
  As men drink potions.   *II. Henry IV.* i. 1.

Fal. I am as poor as Job, my lord, but not so patient; your lordship may minister the potion of imprisonment to me in respect of poverty; but how I should be your patient to follow your prescriptions, the wise may make some dram of a scruple, or, indeed, a scruple itself.   *II. Henry IV.* i. 2.

  Per. Thou speak'st like a physician, Helicanus;
  Who minister'st a potion unto me
  That thou wouldst tremble to receive thyself.
      Pericles, i. 2.

Mixtures.

  Come, phial.—
  What if this mixture do not work at all?
      Romeo and Juliet, iv. 3.

>   I therefore vouch again
> That with some mixtures powerful o'er the blood,
> Or with some dram conjured to this effect,
> He wrought upon her.   *Othello,* i. 3.

Pills.

Fal. Come, let me pour in some sack to the Thames water; for my belly's as cold as if I had swallowed snow-balls for pills to cool the reins. Call her in.   *Merry Wives of Windsor,* iii. 5.

> *Pro.* When I was sick, you gave me bitter pills;
> And I must minister the like to you.
>   *Two Gentlemen of Verona,* ii. 4.

Clysters.

Very good: well kissed! an excellent courtesy! 'tis so, indeed. Yet again your fingers to your lips? would they were clyster-pipes for your sake!   *Othello,* ii. 1.

Cataplasms and *Poultices.* See previous quotation from *Hamlet* (iv. 7), under poisons (p. 55), "No cataplasm so rare."

> Are you so hot? Marry, come up, I trow;
> Is this the poultice for my aching bones?
> Henceforward do your messages yourself.
>   *Romeo and Juliet,* ii. 5.

Salve. (An outward adhesive healing application, including ointments and plasters.)

> A salve for any sore that may betide.
>   *III. Henry VI.* iv. 6.

Plaster occurs in the following beautiful figure:

> *Gon.* My lord Sebastian,
> The truth you speak doth lack some gentleness,
> And time to speak it in; you rub the sore,
> When you should bring the plaster.
> *Seb.* Very well.
> *Ant.* And most chirurgeonly.   *Tempest,* ii. 1.

THERAPEUTICS. No one can fail to observe how wise and reasonable are the views which Shakespeare entertains on the subject of Therapeutics. He neither undervalues nor overestimates the help to be obtained from the administration of medicines. The words of the king in *Cymbeline* epitomize his views :

> But I consider
> By medicine life may be prolong'd, yet death
> Will seize the doctor too.—How ended she?
> *Cymbeline*, v. 5.

Cerimon (*Pericles*, iii. 2) was not only familiar with "the blest infusions that dwell in vegetives, in metals, stones," but he could also "speak of the disturbances that nature works and *of her cures.*" (See p. 72.)

The following passage might seem to countenance a merely expectant mode of treatment :

> *K. Hen.* Then you perceive, the body of our kingdom
> How foul it is ; what rank diseases grow,
> And with what danger near the heart of it.
> *War.* It is but as a body, yet, distemper'd :
> Which to his former strength may be restored,
> With good advice, and little medicine.
> *II. Henry IV*. iii. 1.

But we may set against it this other :

> *Bru.* Sir, those cold ways,
> That seem like prudent helps, are very poisonous
> Where the disease is violent.   *Coriolanus*, iii. 1.

The special therapeutic measures may be considered as diet, regimen, purging, blood-letting, and counter-irritation.

Temperance in diet for the avoidance or curing of disease is inculcated in the following passages :

> *Nor.* What, are you chafed ?
> Ask God for temperance ; that's the appliance only,
> Which your disease requires.   *Henry VIII*. i. 1.

And yet, for aught I see, they are as sick that surfeit with too much, as they that starve with nothing : It is no mean happiness,

therefore, to be seated in the mean ; superfluity comes sooner by white hairs, but competency lives longer.
Merchant of Venice, i. 2.

> For, as a surfeit of the sweetest things
> The deepest loathing to the stomach brings—
> Or, as the heresies, that men do leave,
> Are hated most of those they did deceive:
> So thou, my surfeit, and my heresy,
> Of all be hated ; but the most of me!
> Midsummer-Night's Dream, ii. 2.

> Here am I left to underprop his land ;
> Who, weak with age, cannot support myself :——
> Now comes the sick hour, that his surfeit made ;
> Now shall he try his friends that flatter'd him.
> Richard II. ii. 2.

> *Sec. Lord.* But I am sure, the younger of our nature,
> That surfeit on their ease, will, day by day,
> Come here for physic. *All's Well that Ends Well*, iii. 1.

The advantages of an occasional abstinence from flesh meat are illustrated in Sir Andrew Aguecheek, who says of himself:

> *Sir And.* Never in your life, I think ; unless you see canary put me down. Methinks sometimes I have no more wit than a Christian, or an ordinary man has : but I am a great eater of beef, and I believe that does harm to my wit. *Twelfth Night*, i. 3.

Here we may also notice Petrucio's excuse for throwing away the overdone mutton:

> *Pet.* I tell thee, Kate, 'twas burnt and dried away
> And I expressly am forbid to touch it,
> For it engenders choler, planteth anger ;
> And better 'twere that both of us did fast—
> Since of ourselves, ourselves are choleric—
> Than feed it with such over-roasted flesh.
> Taming of the Shrew, iv. 1.

The advantage of a spare diet to the thinking faculty is tersely put:

> Fat paunches have lean pates; and dainty bits
> Make rich the ribs, but bankrupt quite the wits.
> *Love's Labour's Lost*, i. 1.

With this we may compare Caesar's remarks about Cassius.

> *Caes.* Let me have men about me that are fat:
> Sleek-headed men, and such as sleep o' nights:
> Yond Cassius has a lean and hungry look;
> He thinks too much: such men are dangerous.
> *Julius Caesar*, i. 2.

The treatment by diet in venereal diseases is referred to in *Timon of Athens*, iv. 3. "To the tub-fast and the diet." (See page 95.)

Shakespeare inculcates moderation in other respects also, as where Claudio says:

> *Claud.* From too much liberty, my Lucio, liberty:
> As surfeit is the father of much fast,
> So every scope by the immoderate use
> Turns to restraint. *Measure for Measure*, i. 2.

Purging is often referred to, both literally and as a figure of speech, as in

> Purge him of that humour
> That presses him from sleep. *Winter's Tale*, ii. 3.

> *Fal.* I'll follow, as they say, for reward. He that rewards me, Heaven reward him! If I do grow great, I'll grow less, for I'll purge, and leave sack, and live cleanly, as a nobleman should do.
> *I. Henry IV.* v. 4.

It is used as a figure of speech, in the following passages:

> And with him pour we in our country's purge,
> Each drop of us. *Macbeth*, v. 2.

> Find her disease,
> And purge it to a sound and pristine health.
> *Macbeth*, v. 3.

> Let's purge this choler without letting blood :
> This we prescribe, though no physician ;
> Deep malice makes too deep incision :
> Forget, forgive ; conclude, and be agreed :
> Our doctors say this is no month to bleed.—*Richard II.* i. 1.

> And quietness, grown sick of rest, would purge
> By any desperate change.   *Antony and Cleopatra*, i. 3.

> I take not on me here as a physician :
> Nor do I, as an enemy to peace,
> Troop in the throngs of military men :
> But, rather, show a while like fearful war
> To diet rank minds, sick of happiness ;
> And purge the obstructions,[1] which begin to stop
> Our very veins of life.   *II. Henry IV.* iv. 1.

Blood-letting. A direct reference to this mode of cure occurs in the passage from *Richard II.* i. 1 immediately above quoted, where certain times are indicated as unfavourable for venesection. The other important references to it are the following :

> *Dum.* I would forget her : but a fever she
> Reigns in my blood and will remember'd be.
> *Biron.* A fever in your blood, why, then incision
> Would let her out in saucers ; sweet misprision !
>   *Love's Labour's Lost,* iv. 3.

> *Ros.* Is the fool sick ?
> *Biron.* Sick at heart.
> *Ros.* Alack, let it blood.
> *Biron.* Would that do it good ?
> *Ros.* My physic says, Ay.   *Love's Labour's Lost.* ii. 1.

---

[1] Compare with this phrase the passage :
> Ay, but to die, and go we know not where,
> To lie in cold obstruction, and to rot.
>   *Measure for Measure*, iii. 1.

Dr. Creighton quotes Woodall's *Pathology of Obstructions* in connection with this passage. (*History of Epidemics*, I., p. 605.)

> *Ajax.* I will let his humours blood.
> *Agam.* He'll be physician, that should be the patient.
> *Troilus and Cressida,* ii. 3.

> *Mar.* Sir, praise me not:
> My work hath not yet warmed me: Fare you well.
> The blood I drop is rather physical
> Than dangerous to me. *Coriolanus,* i. 5.

> And with our surfeiting and wanton hours
> Have brought ourselves into a burning fever,
> And we must bleed for it. *II. Henry IV.* iv. 1.

Counter-irritation, and even the violent kind of it sometimes practised in the treatment of inflammation of the eyes, is alluded to in the following passage:

> *Ben.* Tut, man! one fire burns out another's burning,
> One pain is lessen'd by another's anguish:
> Turn giddy, and be holp by backward turning;
> One desperate grief cures with another's languish:
> Take thou some new infection to thy eye,
> And the rank poison of the old will die.
> *Rom.* Your plantain leaf is excellent for that.
> *Ben.* For what, I pray thee?
> *Rom.* For your broken shin. *Romeo and Juliet,* i. 2.

Music as a remedy in madness is spoken of by King Richard as tending to madden him.

> This music mads me, let it sound no more;
> For, though it have holp madmen to their wits,
> In me, it seems, it will make wise men mad.
> *Richard II.* v. 5.

See also the "woful music" referred to under the next heading RESUSCITATION. (*Pericles,* iii. 2.)

The influence of music is referred to by Shakespeare, on the other hand, as the *cause* of a curious morbid symptom. This may be considered here, although it should scarcely be classed under Therapeutics. The passage is in the well-known statement of Shylock's dislike of Antonio:

> Some men there are love not a gaping pig :
> Some, that are mad if they behold a cat ;
> And others, when the bag-pipe sings i' the nose,
> Cannot contain their urine.
>
> . . . .
>
> As there is no firm reason to be render'd,
> Why he cannot abide a gaping pig ;
> Why he, a harmless necessary cat :
> Why he, a bollen bag-pipe ; but of force
> Must yield to such inevitable shame
> As to offend, himself being offended :
> So can I give no reason, nor I will not.
> More than a lodg'd hate and a certain loathing
> I bear Antonio, that I follow thus
> A losing suit against him.   *Merchant of Venice*, iv. 1.

The influence of this form of music in causing incontinence of urine seems to be quite unknown in connection with the sound of the national bagpipes in the Scottish Highlands. The nearest comparable fact appears to be the well-known practice of carters, who often whistle, usually with a long-drawn note, in encouraging their horses to pass urine. The similar influence of the sound of running water on men will be referred to subsequently. The power of the sound of the bagpipe to produce this effect seems to have been proverbial about Shakespeare's time. Ben Jonson says in his play, *Every Man in his Humour* (iv. 1):

> *E. Kn.* What ails thy brother? can he not hold his water at reading of a ballad?
>
> *Well.* O, no ; a rhyme to him is worse than cheese or a bagpipe.

Of medical authority on this point the best known seems to be a statement by Julius Cæsar Scaliger in his book *De Subtilitate* (1612). It occurs in *Exercitatio*, 344, 6, where he discourses on Sympathy. This case of his has passed into various books. The following quotation from the

Hon. Robert Boyle, in his *Essay of the Great Effects of even Languid and Unheeded Motion* (London, 1685, p. 70), gives it in English, with a slight addition of his own at the end, which may be regarded as conforming to a pretty general experience not unfrequently acted on at the present day: "I remember, Scaliger tells a pleasant story of a knight of Gascony, whom the sound of a Bagpipe would force presently to make water; adding, that a person disobliged by this man, and resolving to be merrily revenged on him, watched a time when he sate at a feast so as he could not well get out, and brought a Bagpiper to play unawares behind him, which he did so unluckily, that the musick had presently its wonted effect upon the poor knight, to his great confusion and the laughter of the company. On which occasion I shall add, that I know a very ingenious gentleman who has confessed to me that the noise of a running tap is wont to have almost the like operation upon him."

RESUSCITATION FROM UNCONSCIOUS STATES. When the "caulk'd and bitum'd" chest, containing Pericles' Queen in a state of trance, is washed ashore, we are introduced to Cerimon, a gentleman of fortune who delighted to study diseases and their remedies. His character will be best understood from the following noble sentences about the pursuit of medicine:

> *Cer.* I held it ever,
> Virtue and cunning were endowments greater
> Than nobleness and riches: careless heirs
> May the two latter darken and expend;
> But immortality attends the former,
> Making a man a god. 'Tis known, I ever
> Have studied physic, through which secret art,
> By turning o'er authorities, I have
> (Together with my practice) made familiar
> To me and to my aid, the blest infusions

> That dwell in vegetives, in metals, stones;
> And I can speak of the disturbances
> That nature works, and of her cures; which gives me
> A more content in course of true delight
> Than to be thirsty after tottering honour,
> Or tie my treasure up in silken bags,
> To please the fool and death. *Pericles*, iii. 2.

When the chest is opened Cerimon recognizes that the Queen is in a state of unconsciousness simulating death. The measures taken for her recovery commend themselves as entirely rational and likely to accomplish the object. These are warmth, friction, air,[1] the application of various restoratives (for he orders all the boxes in his closet to be brought), and the stimulation of the nervous system by the sounds of "rough and woful music." Her return to life is beautifully and naturally described:

> If thou livest, Pericles, thou hast a heart
> That even cracks for woe!—This chanced to-night.
>   *Sec. Gent.* Most likely, sir.
>   *Cer.* Nay, certainly to-night;
> For look, how fresh she looks!—They were too rough,
> That threw her in the sea. Make fire within;
> Fetch hither all the boxes in my closet.
> Death may usurp on nature many hours,
> And yet the fire of life kindle again
> The overpressed spirits. I have heard
> Of an Egyptian, had nine hours lien dead,
> By good appliance was recovered.
>
>   *Enter a Servant, with boxes, napkins, and fire.*
> Well said, well said; the fire and the cloths.—
> The rough and woful music that we have,
> Cause it to sound, 'beseech you.
> The vial once more.—How thou stirr'st, thou block!

---

[1] While in the trance air is regarded as unnecessary, but when she awakes the order is given:

> —— I pray you, give her air. *Pericles*, iii. 2.

> The music there.—I pray you, give her air :—
> Gentlemen,
> The queen will live : nature awakes ; a warmth
> Breathes out of her : she hath not been entranced
> Above five hours. See, how she gins to blow
> Into life's flower again!   *Pericles*, iii. 2.

The foolish habit of crowding round a fainting person is turned to metaphorical use by Angelo in *Measure for Measure*, and in the same passage the effect of nervous excitement in disturbing the action of the heart is alluded to. Angelo has already in resolve given way to the temptation, and at the moment when Isabel is announced, he says :

> O Heavens!
> Why does my blood thus muster to my heart,
> Making both it unable for itself,
> And dispossessing all my other parts
> Of necessary fitness?
> So play the foolish throngs with one that swoons ;
> Come all to help him, and so stop the air
> By which he should revive : and even so
> The general, subject to a well-wish'd king,
> Quit their own part, and in obsequious fondness
> Crowd to his presence, where their untaught love
> Must needs appear offence.   *Measure for Measure*, ii. 4.

When Antony announces his intention to depart, Cleopatra, evidently with a premonition of fainting, calls out :

> *Cleo.* Cut my lace, Charmian, come :—
> But let it be.—I am quickly ill and well :
> So Antony loves.   *Antony and Cleopatra*, i. 3.

When King Henry swoons at hearing of Gloster's death, Somerset suggests raising him and wringing him by the nose :

> (*The King swoons.*)
>
> *Q. Mar.* How fares my lord? Help, lords! the king is dead.
> *Som.* Rear up his body ; wring him by the nose.

Q. Mar. Run, go, help, help!—O Henry, ope thine eyes!
Suf. He doth revive again.—Madam, be patient.
II. Henry VI. iii. 2.

The following quotation deserves notice, not so much from the treatment of the swoon as from the metaphor at the close of the passage:

K. Hen. And wherefore should these good news make me sick?
Will Fortune never come with both hands full,
But write her fair words still in foulest letters?
She either gives a stomach and no food,—
Such are the poor, in health; or else a feast,
And takes away the stomach,—such are the rich,
That have abundance, and enjoy it not.
I should rejoice now at this happy news;
And now my sight fails and my brain is giddy:—
O me! come near me; now I am much ill.
[*Swoons.*
P. Humph. Comfort, your majesty!
Cla.   O my royal father!
West. My sovereign lord, cheer up yourself, look up!
War. Be patient, princes; you do know, these fits
Are with his highness very ordinary.
Stand from him, give him air; he'll straight be well.
Cla. No, no, he cannot long hold out these pangs:
Th' incessant care and labour of his mind
Hath wrought the mure, that should confine it in,
So thin, that life looks through, and will break out.
II. Henry IV. iv. 4.

CHAPTER IV

SURGERY

THE surgical ailments which Shakespeare speaks of in his plays are not numerous, and of some the merest mention is made. They include: ABSCESS; BOILS and CARBUNCLES; GANGRENE; FISTULA; WOUNDS and SCARS; FRACTURES and DISLOCATIONS; HARELIP; SQUINT; PIN-and-WEB: VENEREAL DISEASES.

Of the diseases in this list the only one which influences to any extent the action of a play is FISTULA. In the opening scene of *All's Well that Ends Well*, we find the King languishing from a fistula, the cure of which has baffled the efforts of his physicians, so that he was "relinquished of the artists—both of Galen and Paracelsus, of all the learned and authentic fellows—that gave him out incurable, not to be helped—uncertain life and sure death," as announced by Lafeu. (Act ii., Scene 3.) Helena, the daughter of Gerard de Narbon, a distinguished physician, comes to court, and by means of some wonderful "prescriptions of rare and prov'd effects" (i. 3), bequeathed to her by her father on his death-bed, accomplishes the King's cure. The "fistula" here spoken of was not the common form technically called "fistula in ano." On referring to the source from which the plot was obtained, viz. Painter's *Palace of Pleasure*, we find that the "French king had a swelling upon his breast, which, by reason of ill cure, was grown to be a 'fistula,' which did put him to marvellous pain and grief."

A collection of pus in the pleura (technically termed an empyema), which had burst externally and continued to discharge, or possibly a sinus arising from a diseased rib, would agree with the grave constitutional symptoms indicated in the meagre description of the king's ailment. The king is not bedridden, but is able to move about with help. He is subject to attacks of exhaustion, described as "desperate languishes." His physicians have worn him out with several applications, and appear themselves to have lost hope of his improvement, for the King says:

> Our most learned doctors leave us; and
> The congregated college have concluded,
> That labouring art can never ransom nature
> From her inaidable estate.
> *All's Well that Ends Well*, ii. 1.

So far the picture, though wanting in details, is true to nature, but the same can hardly be said of the process of cure. We are not told whether the remedy was to be taken internally or to be applied externally, only that its virtue was so great that the cure was accomplished in two days. The foregoing does not show that Shakespeare possessed any technical knowledge of fistulae and their treatment, but the subject has given him occasion to pen some sayings about medicine which may well excuse the technical ignorance. Among these are the following:

> *Hel.* Our remedies oft in ourselves do lie,
> Which we ascribe to Heaven.   *Ibid.* i. 1.

Then we have Lafeu's statement about the King:

> *Laf.* He hath abandoned his physicians, madam; under whose practices he hath persecuted time with hope; and finds no other advantage in the process but only losing of hope by time. *Ibid.* i. 1.

The King announces his refusal to resort to quackery with due dignity:

> *King.* We thank you, maiden:
> But may not be so credulous of cure,—
> When our most learned doctors leave us; and
> The congregated college have concluded,
> That labouring art can never ransom nature
> From her inaidable estate,—I say, we must not
> So stain our judgment, or corrupt our hope,
> To prostitute our past-cure malady
> To empirics. *Ibid.* ii. 1.

The attitude of mind, so favourable to a cure, to which the King resigns himself when he has resolved to try the remedy, is indicated thus:

> *King.* Here is my hand; the premises observed,
> Thy will by my performance shall be served:
> So make the choice of thy own time; for I,
> Thy resolved patient, on thee still rely.
> More should I question thee, and more I must;
> Though, more to know, could not be more to trust.
> *Ibid.* ii. 1.

Among the other surgical ailments mentioned are BOILS and CARBUNCLES. In the following passage these names are used, but probably the last two refer to the marks of the Plague and not to simple carbuncles. King Lear says to Goneril:

> But yet thou art my flesh, my blood, my daughter;
> Or, rather, a disease that's in my flesh,
> Which I must needs call mine: thou art a boil,
> A plague-sore, an embossed carbuncle,
> In my corrupted blood. *King Lear*, ii. 4.

Again, in the amusing scene with which the second act of *Troilus and Cressida* opens, we read:

Ajax. Thersites,——
Ther. Agamemnon—how if he had boils? full, all over, generally?
Ajax. Thersites,——
Ther. And those boils did run?—Say so,—did not the general run then? Were not that a botchy core?
Ajax. Dog,——
Ther. Then would come some matter from him; I see none now.
Troilus and Cressida, ii. 1.

GANGRENE is spoken of in *Coriolanus*, where Menenius says:

> *Men.* The service of the foot
> Being once gangren'd, is not then respected
> For what before it was.
> *Bru.* We'll hear no more.—
> Pursue him to his house, and pluck him thence:
> Lest his infection, being of catching nature,
> Spread farther. *Coriolanus*, iii. 1.

Again, in *Henry VI.*, Exeter refers to gangrenous processes. The word *sinews* probably includes the nerves:

> As fester'd members rot but by degrees,
> Till bones, and flesh, and sinews, fall away,
> So will this base and envious discord breed.
> *I. Henry VI.* iii. 1.

FRACTURES. The firm repair of broken bones furnishes the following simile:

> And therefore be assured, my good lord marshal,
> If we do now make our atonement well,
> Our peace will, like a broken limb united,
> Grow stronger for the breaking. *II. Henry IV.* iv. 1.

The setting of fractures is humorously referred to by Falstaff:

Well, 'tis no matter: honour pricks me on. Yea, but how if honour prick me off when I come on? how then? Can honour set to

a leg? No. Or an arm? No. Or take away the grief of a wound? No. Honour hath no skill in surgery then? No.
I. Henry IV. v. 1.

ABSCESS. The following metaphor evidently refers to the suppurative process, such as a boil coming to a head:

foul sin, gathering head,
Shall break into corruption. *Richard II.* v. 1.

DISLOCATION. We have this allusion:

Host. No, thou arrant knave; I would I might die, that I might have thee hanged: thou hast drawn my shoulder out of joint.
II. Henry IV. v. 4.

WOUNDS AND SCARS are repeatedly mentioned together, sometimes in a metaphorical sense, as in the well-known line:

Rom. He jests at scars that never felt a wound.
Romeo and Juliet, ii. 2.

More literal applications occur also:

You were advis'd, his flesh was capable
Of wounds and scars. *II. Henry IV.* i. 1.

The more technical term, cicatrices, occurs several times:

Where is he wounded?
Vol. I' the shoulder, and i' the left arm: There will be large cicatrices to shew the people, when he shall stand for his place. He received in the repulse of Tarquin, seven hurts i' the body.
Men. One i' the neck, and two i' the thigh—there's nine that I know. *Coriolanus,* ii. 1.

The appearance of a recently healed wound is referred to metaphorically:

Since yet thy cicatrice looks raw and red. *Hamlet,* iv. 3.

We come upon the following popular beliefs as to wounds:

Patr. O, then beware;
Those wounds heal ill that men do give themselves.
Troilus and Cressida, iii. 3.

This has no doubt some foundation, as the mental condition of those who wilfully wound themselves is one unfavourable to rapid healing.

The use of leeks and their skin is insisted on by the Welsh officer Fluellen, as being good for the healing of wounds. But "eating the leek" was obviously more important for healing the wounded national vanity of the Welshman than for mending Pistol's head:

—Pite, I pray you; it is goot for your green wound, and your ploody coxcomb.

Pist. Must I bite?

. . . .

the skin is goot for your proken coxcomb. *Henry V.* v. 1.

The injurious influence of the air on wounds is mentioned:

> The air hath got into my deadly wounds,
> And much effuse of blood doth make me faint.
> *III. Henry VI.* ii. 6.

If leeks were good for wounds, prawns seem to have been bad:

She had a good dish of prawns; whereby thou didst desire to eat some; whereby I told thee, they were ill for a green wound? *II. Henry IV.* ii. 1.

Promptitude in the treatment of green wounds is recognized as important:

> Send succours, lords, and stop the rage betime,
> Before the wound do grow uncurable.
> For, being green, there is great hope of help.
> *II. Henry VI.* iii. 1.

The belief that the wounds of a murdered man opened and

bled in the presence of his murderer[1] is expressed in the following:

> O gentlemen, see, see! dead Henry's wounds
> Open their congeal'd mouths, and bleed afresh!
> Blush, blush, thou lump of foul deformity:
> For 'tis thy presence that exhales this blood
> From cold and empty *veins*, where no blood dwells:
> Thy deed, inhuman and unnatural,
> Provokes this deluge most unnatural.—
> *Richard III.* i. 2.

The breaking out of wounds afresh is here made use of as a figure of speech:

> The new heal'd wound of malice should break out;
> Which would be so much the more dangerous,
> By how much the estate is green, and yet ungovern'd.
> *Richard III.* ii. 2.

The extension of a wound is spoken of in this curious comparison:

> *Ant.* Thou bleed'st apace.
> *Scar.* I had a wound here that was like a T,
> But now 'tis made an H.   *Antony and Cleopatra,* iv. 7.

It would almost seem as if the practice of having a surgeon present at duels, to prevent unnecessary loss of life, may have been in view in the suggestion that Shylock should have a surgeon at hand to prevent fatal haemorrhage from the carrying out of the penalty claimed:

> *Por.* Have by some surgeon, Shylock, on your charge,
> To stop his wounds, lest he do bleed to death.
> *Merchant of Venice,* iv. 1.

---

[1] King James, in his *Daemonologie*, says: "In a secret murther, if the dead carkasse bee at any time thereafter handled by the murtherer, it will gush out of bloud, as if the bloud were crying to the heauen for reuenge of the murtherer, God hauing appointed that supernaturall signe, for triall of that secret vnnaturall crime."

Nor can we leave this subject without remembering Mercutio's wound :

Mer. No, 'tis not so deep as a well, nor so wide as a church-door; but 'tis enough, 'twill serve: ask for me to-morrow and you shall find me a grave man. I am peppered, I warrant, for this world :— A plague o' both your houses !—Zounds, a dog, a rat, a mouse, a cat, to scratch a man to death ! a braggart, a rogue, a villain, that fights by the book of arithmetic !—Why the devil came you between us ? I was hurt under your arm. *Romeo and Juliet*, iii. 1.

ULCERS. Under this heading we may notice the "King's Evil," which Shakespeare introduces in *Macbeth*. The Royal Touch is described by Malcolm, after the conversation between him and Macduff:

Enter a Doctor.
Mal. Well; more anon.—Comes the king forth, I pray you ?
Doct. Ay, sir: there are a crew of wretched souls,
That stay his cure: their malady convinces
The great assay of art; but, at his touch,
Such sanctity hath Heaven given his hand,
They presently amend.
Mal. I thank you, doctor. [*Exit Doctor.*
Macd. What's the disease he means ?
Mal. 'Tis called the evil:
A most miraculous work in this good king;
Which often, since my here-remain in England,
I have seen him do. How he solicits Heaven,
Himself best knows: but strangely-visited people
All swoln and ulcerous, pitiful to the eye,
The mere despair of surgery, he cures;
Hanging a golden stamp about their necks,
Put on with holy prayers: and 'tis spoken,
To the succeeding royalty he leaves
The healing benediction. With this strange virtue
He hath a heavenly gift of prophecy;
And sundry blessings hang about his throne,
That speak him full of grace. *Macbeth*, iv. 3.

In the Doctor's speech "convinces" (as in some other passages in Shakespeare) must be understood as meaning "vanquishes." We can readily understand his speaking of the swellings and ulcerations of scrofula as vanquishing the effort of medical art.

The superficial healing of a sore, which had not filled up from the bottom, supplies Hamlet with this fine metaphor:

> Mother, for love of grace,
> Lay not that flattering unction to your soul,
> That not your trespass, but my madness, speaks:
> It will but skin and film the ulcerous place;
> Whiles rank corruption, mining all within,
> Infects unseen. *Hamlet*, iii. 4.

HARELIP.—SQUINT. These two are coupled in the insane sayings of Edgar when he simulates madness. Speaking of "the foul fiend Flibbertigibbet," he says:

> He gives the web and the pin, squints the eye,
> And makes the hare-lip. *King Lear*, iii. 4.

THE WEB AND THE PIN, mentioned in the last quotation, is the same as "pin-and-web" in the next passage. It was a name for opacities of the cornea, and it included the opacity of cataract also:[1]

> And all eyes
> Blind with the pin-and-web, but their's, their's only,
> That would unseen be wicked. *Winter's Tale*, i. 2.

(See also Chapter v. under *Congenital Defects*, etc.)

The modes of SURGICAL TREATMENT to which allusion is made are: INCISIONS, AMPUTATIONS, CAUTERIZING, USING TENTS, SETONS or ISSUES.

---

[1] See Peter Lowe's *Chirurgerie*. Lond. 1612. Lib. v. (chap. 19), "Of the web in the eye," etc.

INCISIONS, by lancing, are referred to:

> Fell sorrow's tooth doth never rankle more,
> Than when it bites, but lanceth not the sore.
> *Richard II.* i. 3.

> But we do lance
> Diseases in our bodies. *Antony and Cleopatra*, v. 1.

AMPUTATIONS. The danger of amputation, and the possibility of cure without such an extreme measure, are here made use of:

> *Sic.* He's a disease that must be cut away.
> *Men.* O, he's a limb, that has but a disease;
> Mortal, to cut it off; to cure it, easy. *Coriolanus*, iii. 1.

On the other hand, the doctrine of "cut it off, and cast it from thee," is equally admitted:

> This fester'd joint cut off, the rest rests sound;
> This, let alone, will all the rest confound.
> *Richard II.* v. 3.

CAUTERIZING, or the use of corrosive caustics, may be found mentioned in the following:

> *Q. Mar.* Away! though parting be a fretful corrosive,
> It is applied to a deathful wound. *II. Henry VI.* iii. 2.

> Care is no cure, but rather corrosive,
> For things that are not to be remedied.
> *I. Henry VI.* iii. 3.

> For each true word, a blister! and each false
> Be as a caut'rizing to the root o' the tongue,
> Consuming it with speaking! *Timon of Athens*, v. 1.

TENTS were pledgets of lint, medicated or otherwise, introduced into wounds and abscesses to promote a healthy, healing action.

> *Patr.* Who keeps the tent now?
> *Ther.* The surgeon's box, or the patient's wound.
> *Troilus and Cressida*, v. 1.

SURGERY

    Leave us to cure this cause.
     Men. For 'tis a sore upon us,
    You cannot tent yourself: Begone, 'beseech you.
                               Coriolanus, iii. 1.

    Mar. I have some wounds upon me, and they smart
To hear themselves remember'd.
    Com. Should they not,
Well might they fester 'gainst ingratitude,
And tent themselves with death.   *Coriolanus*, i. 9.

    Imo. Talk thy tongue weary; speak:
I have heard, I am a strumpet; and mine ear,
Therein false struck, can take no greater wound,
Nor tent to bottom that.   *Cymbeline*, iii. 4.

    I'll observe his looks;
I'll tent him to the quick; if he do blench,
I know my course.   *Hamlet*, ii. 2.

    The wound of peace is surety,
Surety secure; but modest doubt is call'd
The beacon of the wise, the tent, that searches
To the bottom of the worst.   *Troilus and Cressida*, ii. 2.

SETONS or ISSUES may be referred to in the following passage:

    I am not glad, that such a sore of time
Should seek a plaster by contemn'd revolt,
And heal the inveterate canker of one wound,
By making many.   *King John*, v. 2.

Possibly, however, the "plaster" referred to may refer to a blistering plaster to produce counter-irritation.

    RESTRAINING HAEMORRHAGE. Two modes of accomplishing this are given. Both depend for their efficacy on their causing coagulation of the blood by bringing into contact with it fine filaments—in the one case of cobweb and in the other of flax. The former method remains a popular tradition to this day.

Bot. I shall desire you of more acquaintance, good master Cobweb: If I cut my finger, I shall make bold with you.—
Midsummer-Night's Dream, iii. 1.

Third Serv. Go thou; I'll fetch some flax, and whites of eggs,
To apply to his bleeding face. Now, Heaven help him!
King Lear, iii. 7.

VENEREAL DISEASES.

The century preceding Shakespeare's era witnessed the rapid spread of syphilis throughout Europe; this followed the siege of Naples. That the occurrence of this disease was frequent and its symptoms familiar, we may learn from the form of vulgar oath which Shakespeare puts into the mouth of many of his characters, and into none more appropriately than into that of Falstaff (see p. 37):

A pox of this gout! or, a gout of this pox!
II. Henry IV. i. 2.

The interpretation of this frequent oath as referring to the disease now termed small-pox cannot be admitted as probable. No doubt "variole" (our small-pox) was called "the poxe," and the ambiguity of this word may have rendered it possible for the current oath to be used with less sense of shame, as where Katharine says:

A pox of that jest! *Love's Labour's Lost*, v. 2.

Many jesting allusions occur to symptoms of syphilis, as in the following. The baldness (alopecia) produced by this disease came to be known as the "French crown," and the play on the word "crown," as a piece of money, explains the joke:

Lucio. Behold, behold, where Madame Mitigation comes!
First Gent. I have purchased as many diseases under her roof as come to——

SURGERY

>*Sec. Gent.* To what, I pray?
>*First Gent.* Judge.
>*Sec. Gent.* To three thousand dolours a year.
>*First Gent.* Ay, and more.
>*Lucio.* A French crown more.   *Measure for Measure*, i. 2.

Again:

>*Bot.* I will discharge it in either your straw-colour beard, your orange-tawny beard, your purple-in-grain beard, or your French-crown-colour beard, your perfect yellow.
>*Quin.* Some of your French crowns have no hair at all, and then you will play barefaced.   *Midsummer-Night's Dream*, i. 2.

Again:

>*K. Hen.* Indeed, the French may lay twenty French crowns to one, they will beat us; for they bear them on their shoulders: but it is no English treason to cut French crowns, and to-morrow the king himself will be a clipper.   *King Henry V.* iv. 1.

The term "pocky corses" used by the Clown in *Hamlet* refers to this form of pox and not to small-pox:

>*First Clo.* I' faith, if he be not rotten before he die,—as we have many pocky corses now-a-days that will scarce hold the laying in,—he will last you some eight year, or nine year: a tanner will last you nine year.   *Hamlet*, v. 1.

These quotations serve to show the widespread knowledge of the disease and its symptoms amongst the common people in Shakespeare's plays. A more subtle allusion occurs, probably, in the question already quoted (p. 29):

>*First Gent.* How now! which of your hips has the most profound sciatica?   *Measure for Measure*, i. 2.

This is addressed to Mistress Overdone, and immediately follows the passage quoted above about the "French crown."

The question as to whether venereal diseases should be treated by physicians or surgeons was hotly disputed in France; both sections of the profession were unwilling to see such a lucrative department of work slipping out of their hands. In *Pericles* we seem to find that the cure of such disorders fell to the surgeon :

Lys. You may say so ; 'tis better for you that your resorters stand upon sound legs. How now, wholesome iniquity ? Have you that a man may deal withal, and defy the surgeon ?
Pericles, iv. 6.

The designation of syphilis as the "French disease" (Morbus Gallicus) was current throughout Europe, although those in France might prefer the name Spanish ("Spanish sickness") or the Neapolitan disease. In connection with this we find the following :

Pist. Doth fortune play the huswife with me now ? News have I that my Nell is dead i' the spital of malady of France.
Henry V. v. 1.

In *Troilus and Cressida* Thersites says :

After this, the vengeance on the whole camp ! or rather, the bone-ache ! for that, methinks, is a curse dependant on those that war for a placket. *Troilus and Cressida*, ii. 3.

In this passage the Quarto has "*the* Neopolitan *bone-ache.*" This makes the allusion more definite, although the word "placket" is itself sufficiently suggestive.

A similar reference to the spread of the disease from Naples occurs in the discourse of the Clown with the musicians in *Othello*. The allusion is to the alterations in the nose, thereby affecting the voice, produced by syphilis; it is applied, metaphorically, in finding fault with the wind instruments of the musicians :

Clo. Why, masters, have your instruments been in Naples, that they speak i' the nose thus ? *Othello*, iii. 1.

The more severe forms of syphilitic disease, its chief symptoms, its treatment, and its mode of communication, all receive mention in the plays.

The most remarkable of these passages occur in that powerful play, *Timon of Athens*, in which the horrors of this disease are made use of to deepen our sense of the intensity of Timon's hatred of and contempt for humanity.

In the curse which Timon flings at his flatterers, at his farewell banquet, occurs the passage:

>Of man and beast the infinite maladie
>Crust you quite o'er!— *Timon of Athens*, iii. 6.

This refers to syphilitic rupia, or some of the scaly syphilitic eruptions. When he finds the gold in the earth he says:

>This yellow slave
>Will knit and break religions; bless the accursed;
>Make the hoar leprosy adored; place thieves,
>And give them title, knee, and approbation,
>With senators on the bench: this is it,
>That makes the wappen'd widow wed again;
>She, whom the spital-house, and ulcerous sores
>Would cast the gorge at, this embalms and spices
>To the April day again. *Timon of Athens*, iv. 3.

"Wappen'd" here means decayed or diseased, and taken in connection with the lines following, little doubt is left as to what disease is implied.

We have the following passage following closely on the one last quoted, in which syphilitic disease is further referred to, and in the phrase, "burn him up," some reference to gonorrhoea may, perhaps, be traced:

>I'll trust to your conditions: Be whores still;
>And he whose pious breath seeks to convert you,
>Be strong in whore, allure him, burn him up;
>Let your close fire predominate his smoke,
>And be no turncoats: Yet may your pains, six months,
>Be quite contrary: And thatch your poor thin roofs
>With burdens of the dead;—some that were hang'd,

> No matter;—wear them, betray with them: whore still,
> Paint, till a horse may mire upon your face:
> A pox of wrinkles! *Timon of Athens*, iv. 3.

The meaning of the phrase, "Yet may your pains, six months, be quite contrary," is somewhat obscure. It may be understood by taking the word "contrary" to mean "repugnant to," a significance which, in old authors, it sometimes bears. The "six months" would thus refer to the average duration of the exanthematous stage of the disease, and some colour is given to this by the suggestions which immediately follow, to supply the loss of hair by the wearing of a wig, and to hide the cutaneous appearances by painting the face.

On the courtezans asking for more gold, Timon tells them what he would further have them do:

> *Tim.* Consumptions sow
> In hollow bones of man; strike their sharp shins,
> And mar men's spurring. Crack the lawyer's voice,
> That he may never more false title plead,
> Nor sound his quillets shrilly: hoar the flamen,
> That scolds against the quality of flesh,
> And not believes himself: down with the nose,
> Down with it flat; take the bridge quite away
> Of him that, his particular to foresee,
> Smells from the general weal: make curl'd-pate ruffians bald:
> And let the unscarr'd braggarts of the war
> Derive some pain from you: Plague all;
> That your activity may defeat and quell
> The source of all erection.—There's more gold:—
> Do you damn others, and let this damn you,
> And ditches grave you all! *Timon of Athens*, iv. 3.

In this passage the lesions which are referred to are those of the tertiary stage. We have first the periosteal nodes which often proceed to suppuration, and the tibia, or shin bone, is indicated as being their favourite seat. Next are mentioned the effects on the voice of tertiary ulcerations of the throat and larynx. "Hoar the flamen" means "make the priest grey"; it may be intended to depict the general ravages of the disease or some particular cutaneous eruption. In the next sentence is mentioned the characteristic facial appearance of tertiary syphilis produced by exfoliation of the nasal bones. Next comes syphilitic alopecia or baldness, followed by tertiary ulcerations of the skin, which would mark with cicatrices those who had escaped that honour in the war. The passage from "Plague all" does not allude to any special lesion, but is the expression of the wish that the disease may spread so universally in its loathsome forms as to quench even the sexual appetite.

Syphilitic affections of the bones are mentioned also in this passage:

First Gent. Thou art always figuring diseases in me: but thou art full of error; I am sound.

Lucio. Nay, not as one would say, healthy; but so sound, as things that are hollow; thy bones are hollow: impiety has made a feast of thee. *Measure for Measure*, i. 2.

The "bone-ache" has been already mentioned in connection with the name Neapolitan (*Troilus and Cressida*, ii. 3, see p. 88). With the adjective "incurable" prefixed, it has also been mentioned in a list of diseases, many, if not all of which, are selected as being results of the "rotten diseases of the South" (*Troilus and Cressida*, v. 1, see p. 17).

When Iachimo slanders Posthumus to Imogen, he refers to venereal diseases in the following terms:

A lady
So fair, and fasten'd to an empery,
Would make the great'st king double! to be partner'd
With tomboys, hired with that self exhibition,
Which your own coffers yield! with diseased ventures,

> That play with all infirmities for gold,
> Which rottenness can lend nature; such boil'd stuff,
> As well might poison poison! *Cymbeline*, i. 6.

Regarding the treatment of venereal diseases, mercury had been introduced as a remedy for syphilis many years before Shakespeare wrote, but no allusion to it can be traced in any of the plays. Baths and the "tub," however, are mentioned several times, and also the "powdering-tub." The treatment by a very strict regimen or diet is also mentioned, sometimes with the "tub," sometimes alone. The cure by sweating, no doubt somewhat connected with the "tub," is also referred to. Pistol says:

> No; to the spital go,
> And from the powdering-tub of infamy
> Fetch forth the lazar kite of Cressid's kind,
> Doll Tearsheet she by name, and her espouse.
> *King Henry V.* ii. 1.

Again:

Lucio. How doth my dear morsel, thy mistress? Procures she still, ha?

Pom. Troth, sir, she hath eaten up all her beef, and she is herself in the tub. *Measure for Measure*, iii. 2.

When the two courtezans, with Alcibiades, visit Timon, speaking to one of them he mentions "tubs and baths," and "the tub-fast and the diet," among the cures for venereal disease:

> *Tim.* Be a whore still! they love thee not that use thee;
> Give them diseases, leaving with thee their lust.
> Make use of thy salt hours: season the slaves
> For tubs and baths; bring down rose-cheeked youth
> To the tub-fast and the diet. *Timon of Athens*, iv. 3.

The treatment by diet alone is mentioned by Pompey in this passage:

SURGERY

Pom. Why, very well: I telling you then, if you be remember'd, that such a one, and such a one, were past cure of the thing you wot of, unless they kept very good diet, as I told you.
Measure for Measure, ii. 1.

The cure by sweating is thus referred to:

> Till then I'll sweat, and seek about for eases;
> And, at that time, bequeath you my diseases.
Troilus and Cressida, v. 10.

The following allusion to the danger of concealing "a foul disease," and so aggravating the danger, may refer to this common aggravation of venereal affections, although possibly it is intended to have a more general reference. In connection with the treatment of such cases it seems worth quoting here:

> But like the owner of a foul disease,
> To keep it from divulging, let it feed
> Even on the pith of life.   *Hamlet*, iv. 1.

The propagation of the contagion of syphilis is repeatedly referred to. Marina says:

> For me
> That am a maid, though most ungentle fortune
> Have plac'd me in this sty, where, since I came,
> Diseases have been sold dearer than physic.
Pericles, iv. 6.

Falstaff also expounds the matter:

Fal. You make fat rascals, mistress Doll.
Doll. I make them! Gluttony and diseases make them; I make them not.
Fal. If the cook help to make the gluttony, you help to make the diseases, Doll: we catch of you, Doll, we catch of you; grant that, my poor virtue, grant that.   *II. Henry IV.* ii. 4.

Probably the infection by kissing is alluded to in this passage. The phrase, "Thy lips rot off," is a curse without special significance of this kind, but it is taken up by Timon :

> This fell whore of thine
> Hath in her more destruction than thy sword,
> For all her cherubin look.
> *Phry.* Thy lips rot off!
> *Tim.* I will not kiss thee: then the rot returns
> To thine own lips again. *Timon of Athens,* iv. 3.

There is also probably an allusion to the idea current then, and even now, that venereal disease may be got rid of by transferring it to a healthy subject.

The danger of the lips, and the contamination of the cup, are probably referred to by Lucio :

> But whilst I live, forget to drink after thee.
> *Measure for Measure,* i. 2.

Occasionally there are allusions to gonorrhoea as a special form of venereal disease (see p. 89), and the curse of a "burning devil" probably refers to this :

> Lechery, lechery: still, wars and lechery: nothing else holds fashion: a burning devil take them! *Troilus and Cressida,* v. 2.

This disease was called the "Brenning" or Burning (see Murray's *English Dictionary*), and so the word lent itself to various puns. Thus in the *Comedy of Errors* we find :

Dro. S. Master, is this Mistress Satan?
Ant. S. It is the devil.
Dro. S. Nay, she is worse, she is the devil's dam: and here she comes in the habit of a light wench: and thereof comes that the wenches say "God damn me"; that's as much as to say, "God make me a light wench." It is written, they appear to men like angels of light: light is an effect of fire, and fire will burn: *ergo*, light wenches will burn. Come not near her.
Comedy of Errors, iv. 3.

In a similar manner Falstaff makes out that one of the women (Doll), inquired about by the Prince, is even now in Hell, as she already "burns," *i.e.* is affected with the "Brenning."

P. Hen. For the women?
Fal. For one of them,—she is in hell already, and burns, poor soul! For the other,—I owe her money: and whether she is damned for that, I know not.
Host. No, I warrant you. *II. Henry IV.* ii. 4.

NOTE.

"The powdering tub of infamy" (*Henry V.* ii. 1). "The tub-fast and the diet."—"Season the slaves for tubs and baths" (*Timon of Athens*, iv. 3). "She has eaten up all her beef, and she is herself in the tub."—"Ever your fresh whore and your powdered bawd" (*Measure for Measure*, iii. 2).

These phrases refer to the treatment of the French disease by means of the "tub." This was essentially a treatment by sweating, although it was associated also with medication. It was familiarly spoken of as "Cornelius' tub," but why it was called so remains obscure. Halliwell, in his notes on these "tub" passages in Shakespeare, gives an amusing extract from Davenant's "Platonick Lover" (1636), in which we find the humorous suggestion thrown out that some ignorant apothecary, by confusing Diogenes and Cornelius, had given rise to the name; the former, it was said, "fasted much and took his habitation in a tub, to make the world believe he lived a strict and severe life, he took the diet, sir, and in that very tub swet for the French disease." As Halliwell says, this is not a serious explanation, but a pleasantry: it is doubtful, however, if it is one which the ancient cynic would have appreciated if he could have foreseen it.

The following extract from Bullein gives an account of the method of cure referred to. The tub ordered by him is a "woodden vessel," and it seems to have been the same kind of tub as that used for curing or corning meat; the meat was powdered or sprinkled with salt in the process, and so the tub used for this purpose was actually called a "powdering-tub." This explains the phrase in *Measure for Measure*, "She hath eaten up all her beef, and she is herself in the tub": it probably also explains the term, "powdering-tub of infamy".—"the powdering-tub" for curing meat becoming a "tub of infamy" when used for curing the French disease. It is true we find Bullein ordering certain herbs to be powdered or "ground" and put into the tub; but the other idea probably supplies the real meaning of the word "powdering": the phrase, "ever your fresh whore and your powdered bawd," seems by the antithesis to confirm this view.

In the section, "A treatise of the pockes," Bullein gives full directions for the cure of the French disease, especially by the use of guaiacum: the last direction concerns the use of the "tub":

Eightly, after ix. or x. dayes be past, once in three dayes let the sicke bodye bee bathed on this sort. Set fayre running water on the fyre, and put therto a great deale of ground Ivie leaves, and red Sage and Fenell also, and by a good fyre when the sicke body is going to Bed, put the water and herbes into a vessell of wood, and let the sicke Body stand upryght in it, by the fyre, and take up the herbes and rubbe the body of the sicke Pacient dounewards, and then dry him with warme cloathes, use this, iii. weekes, and by the grace of God the sicke body shalbe made whole, etc., etc.

During this treatment Bullein seems less strict in his diet than some; but he says: "Also the sicke body must eate but little meate, and that kynde of meate as shall here after be prescribed, and at sutch time as shalbe appoynted."—Bullein: *Bulwarke of Defence.* London, 1579. *Booke of Compoundes.* Folio 43.

Owing to the strict diet prescribed during the "tub" treatment, it was termed the "tub-fast." A treatment by "diet" only or chiefly was also practised, and so we have the curious combination "the tub-fast and the diet." The "tub" is referred to apart from the "diet" in two passages quoted above; and the "diet" is also referred to apart from the "tub" (*Measure for Measure*, ii. 1).

CHAPTER V

MIDWIFERY

THE subjects connected with the Art of Midwifery which are mentioned in the plays include the following: PREMATURE BIRTHS, QUICKENING, ALTERED APPETITE OF PREGNANCY, DEFORMITY OF THE FOETUS, ERUPTION OF TEETH BEFORE BIRTH, DEATH OF FOETUS AND ITS RETENTION IN UTERO, RETARDED LABOUR FROM DEFORMITY OF CHILD, FOOT PRESENTATION, CAESARIAN SECTION, TWIN BIRTHS, SUCKLING, WEANING.

There are two PREMATURE BIRTHS recorded, which have an important influence on the action of the play. One of these occurs in *Pericles*. In the third act Gower tells how the Prince is compelled to journey by sea to Tyre, and how his Queen, whose confinement is " well-a-near," resolves to accompany him. The vessel is overtaken by a storm, and the fear into which the Queen falls brings on premature labour, resulting in the birth of a daughter and the apparent death of the Queen. The story which follows, of the Queen being imprisoned in a water-tight chest, washed ashore, and afterwards resuscitated, has evidently been taken by Shakespeare from the original source of the play, without consideration of its violation of natural laws. With this we are not concerned at present, our interest being confined to the induction of premature labour by the rolling of the ship and the fear of the storm: and the prayer of Pericles in the first scene, which he closes in these words:

> —Lucina, O
> Divinest patroness, and midwife, gentle
> To those that cry by night, convey thy deity
> Aboard our dancing boat; make swift the pangs
> Of my queen's travails!— *Pericles*, iii. 1.

The other premature birth occurs in *Winter's Tale*, where the Queen Hermione is cast into prison close upon her confinement. On Paulina inquiring for the Queen, the nurse tells her how the Queen fares:

> *Emil.* As well as one so great, and so forlorn,
> May hold together: on her frights and griefs,
> (Which never tender lady hath borne greater,)
> She is, something before her time, deliver'd.
> *Paul.* A boy?
> *Emil.* A daughter; and a goodly babe,
> Lusty, and like to live: the queen receives
> Much comfort in 't; says, *My poor prisoner,*
> *I am innocent as you.* *Winter's Tale*, ii. 2.

Here also the poet required for his play the birth of a living child, and so the labour comes on shortly before the full time. The causes of the premature birth are in this case, as in the previous one, fear and grief.

Another recognition of mental emotion as sufficient even to cause the death of the foetus, occurs where Queen Elizabeth, on hearing that Edward was taken prisoner, says:

> And I the rather wean me from despair,
> For love of Edward's offspring in my womb:
> This is it that makes me bridle passion,
> And bear with mildness my misfortune's cross;

> Ay, ay, for this I draw in many a tear,
> And stop the rising of blood-sucking sighs,
> Lest with my sighs or tears I blast or drown
> King Edward's fruit, true heir to the English crown.
>
> *III. Henry VI.* iv. 4.

ABORTIONS. Lady Anne, invoking a curse on Gloster, the murderer of Henry, says:

> If ever he have child, abortive be it,
> Prodigious, and untimely brought to light,
> Whose ugly and unnatural aspect
> May fright the hopeful mother at the view;
> And that be heir to his unhappiness! *Richard III.* i. 2.

The influence of physical violence in causing miscarriage is referred to in the following passage:

Doll. Nut-hook, nut-hook, you lie. Come on; I'll tell thee what, thou damned tripe-visaged rascal; an the child I now go with, do miscarry, thou wert better thou hadst struck thy mother, thou paper-faced villain.

Host. O the Lord that Sir John were come! he would make this a bloody day to somebody. But I pray God the fruit of her womb may miscarry! *II. Henry IV.* v. 4.

ILLEGITIMACY PROVED BY THE DATE OF PREGNANCY. When Faulconbridge is arguing that his brother is illegitimate, he refers to his father's death-bed statement:

> And took it on his death,
> That this, my mother's son, was none of his;
> And, if he were, he came into the world
> Full fourteen weeks before the course of time.
>
> *King John*, i. 2.

And it is interesting to note that the "*fourteen*" weeks named by Shakespeare makes the supposition of his being a son of Sir Robert prematurely born impossible, as it makes his birth take place in the "non-viable" period of pregnancy.

DEFORMITIES AT BIRTH. Richard III. speaks of himself as prematurely born.

> I, that am curtail'd of this fair proportion,
> Cheated of feature by dissembling nature,
> Deform'd, unfinish'd, sent before my time
> Into this breathing world, scarce half made up,
> And that so lamely and unfashionable,
> That dogs bark at me, as I halt by them.
> *Richard III.* i. 1.

There are other peculiarities about his birth which it is convenient to notice here. In the following passage he describes fully his congenital deformities:

> Why, love forswore me in my mother's womb:
> And, for I should not deal in her soft laws,
> She did corrupt frail nature with some bribe
> To shrink mine arm up like a withered shrub,
> To make an envious mountain on my back,
> Where sits deformity to mock my body:
> To shape my legs of an unequal size;
> To disproportion me in every part,
> Like to a chaos, or an unlick'd bear-whelp,
> That carries no impression like the dam.
> *III. Henry VI.* iii. 2.

ERUPTION OF THE TEETH BEFORE BIRTH, FOOT PRESENTATION, and RETARDING OF LABOUR FROM DEFORMITY OF THE CHILD. All these are exemplified in Richard's birth, as witnessed by the following passages:

> From forth the kennel of thy womb hath crept
> A hell-hound that doth hunt us all to death:
> That dog that had his teeth before his eyes,
> To worry lambs, and lap their gentle blood;
> That foul defacer of God's handy-work.
> *Richard III.* iv. 4.

> For I have often heard my mother say,
> I came into the world with my legs forward:

> Had I not reason, think ye, to make haste,
> And seek their ruin that usurp'd our right?
> The midwife wonder'd; and the women cried,
> *O Jesus bless us, he is born with teeth!*"
>
> III. Henry VI. v. 6.

> Thy mother felt more than a mother's pain,
> And yet brought forth less than a mother's hope,
> To wit,—an indigest deformed lump,
> Not like the fruit of such a goodly tree.
> Teeth hadst thou in thy head, when thou wast born,
> To signify,—thou camest to bite the world.
>
> III. Henry VI. v. 6.

THE DEATH OF THE FOETUS and its retention in the womb, are indicated in the excuse put forward by Henry VIII. for one of his divorces.

> First, methought,
> I stood not in the smile of heaven: who had
> Commanded nature, that my lady's womb,
> If it conceived a male child by me, should
> Do no more offices of life to't, than
> The grave does to the dead; for her male issue
> Or died where they were made, or shortly after
> This world had air'd them. *Henry VIII.* ii. 4.

QUICKENING is described by the Clown as follows:

Cost. Faith, unless you play the honest Trojan, the poor wench is cast away: she's quick; the child brags in her belly already; 'tis yours. *Love's Labour's Lost*, v. 2.

The following is clearly a reference to the ALTERED APPETITE OF PREGNANCY:

Clo. Sir, she came in great with child; and longing (saving your honour's reverence) for stew'd prunes; sir, we had but two in the house, which at that very distant time stood, as it were, in a fruit-dish, a dish of some three pence; your honours have seen such dishes; they are not China dishes, but very good dishes.

Measure for Measure, ii. 1.

LABOUR. The birth of Elizabeth in the play of *Henry VIII.* is spoken of as a difficult labour. Lovell tells the Bishop of Winchester that

>   The queen's in labour,
> They say, in great extremity; and fear'd,
> She'll with the labour end.   *Henry VIII.* v. 1.

Later, in the same scene, the King makes inquiries:

> Now, Lovell, from the queen what is the news?
>   *Lov.* I could not personally deliver to her
> What you commanded me, but by her woman
> I sent your message; who returned her thanks
> In the greatest humbleness, and desired your highness
> Most heartily to pray for her.
>   *K. Hen.* What say'st thou? ha!
> To pray for her? what, is she crying out?
>   *Lov.* So said her woman; and that her sufferance made
> Almost each pang à death.
>   *K. Hen.* Alas, good lady!
>   *Suf.* God safely quit her of her burden, and
> With gentle travail.   *Henry VIII.* v. 1.

The fortunate termination of the case we learn of from the amusing passage with which the scene closes:

> I guess thy message. Is the queen deliver'd?
> Say, ay; and of a boy.
>   *Lady.* Ay, ay, my liege;
> And of a lovely boy: The God of Heaven
> Both now and ever bless her!—'tis a girl,
> Promises boys hereafter. Sir, your queen
> Desires your visitation, and to be
> Acquainted with this stranger; 'tis as like you
> As cherry is to cherry.
>   *K. Hen.* Lovell,—
>   *Enter* LOVELL.
>   *Lov.* Sir.
>   *K. Hen.* Give her an hundred marks. I'll to the queen.
>   [*Exit King.*

> *Lady.* An hundred marks! By this light, I'll have more.
> An ordinary groom is for such payment.
> I will have more, or scold it out of him.
> Said I for this, the girl is like to him?
> I will have more, or else unsay't; and now
> While it is hot, I'll put it to the issue.
> *Henry VIII.* v. 1.

The following passages refer to the physical suffering and the cries and groans which are the ordinary accompaniments of parturition:

> *Duch.* Had'st thou groan'd for him,
> As I have done, thou'dst be more pitiful.
> But now I know thy mind: thou dost suspect,
> That I have been disloyal to thy bed,
> And that he is a bastard, not thy son:
> Sweet York, sweet husband, be not of that mind:
> He is as like thee as a man may be,
> Not like to me, or any of my kin,
> And yet I love him. *Richard II.* v. 2.

Beat. No, sure, my lord, my mother cried; but then there was a star danced, and under that was I born.—Cousins, God give you joy!
Much Ado about Nothing, ii. 1.

> *Prov.* I crave your honour's pardon.—
> What shall be done, sir, with the groaning Juliet?
> She's very near her hour. *Measure for Measure,* ii. 2.

> Hadst thou but loved him half so well as I,
> Or felt that pain which I did for him once,
> Or nourish'd him as I did with my blood,
> Thou wouldst have left thy dearest heart-blood there,
> Rather than made that savage duke thine heir,
> And disinherited thine only son. *III. Henry VI.* i. 1.

> But, that I am as well begot, my liege,
> (Fair fall the bones that took the pains for me!)
> Compare our faces and be judge yourself.
> *King John,* i. 1.

Can. With news the time's with labour; and throes forth Each minute some. *Antony and Cleopatra,* iii. 7.

> *Queen.* So, Green, thou art the midwife to my woe,
> And Bolingbroke my sorrow's dismal heir:
> Now hath my soul brought forth her prodigy,
> And I, a gasping new-deliver'd mother,
> Have woe to woe, sorrow to sorrow join'd.
> *Richard II.* ii. 2.

CAESARIAN SECTION furnishes the device in *Macbeth* by which, though slain by Macduff, Macbeth yields not his life to one of woman born. Tradition had invested the birth of Macduff with this incident.

> *Macb.* Thou losest labour:
> As easy may'st thou the intrenchant air
> With thy keen sword impress, as make me bleed:
> Let fall thy blade on vulnerable crests;
> I bear a charmed life, which must not yield
> To one of woman born.
>   *Macd.* Despair thy charm;
> And let the angel whom thou still hast served,
> Tell thee, Macduff was from his mother's womb
> Untimely ripp'd.
> *Macbeth*, v. 7.

TWIN BIRTHS are referred to in the following passages:

>   Till my factor's death,
> And the great care of goods at random left,
> Drew me from kind embracements of my spouse:
> From whom my absence was not six months old,
> Before herself (almost at fainting under
> The pleasing punishment that women bear)
> Had made provision for her following me,
> And soon, and safe, arrived where I was.
> There she had not been long, but she became
> A joyful mother of two goodly sons.
>
> . . . .
>
> That very hour and in the self-same inn,
> A meaner woman was delivered
> Of such a burden, male twins, both alike.
> *Comedy of Errors*, i. 1.

> And he that is approved in this offence,
> Though he had twinn'd with me, both at a birth,
> Shall lose me. *Othello,* ii. 3.

> Twinn'd brothers of one womb,
> Whose procreation, residence, and birth,
> Scarce is dividant,—touch them with several fortunes;
> The greater scorns the lesser. *Timon of Athens,* iv. 3.

> *Cade.* By her, he had two children at one birth.
> *W. Staf.* That's false.
> *Cade.* Ay, there's the question; but, I say, 'tis true.
> *II. Henry VI.* iv. 2.

THE NEW-BORN BABE. Its cry is most aptly made use of by poor King Lear:

> Thou must be patient; we came crying hither.
> Thou know'st the first time that we smell the air,
> We wawl, and cry:—I will preach to thee; mark me.
> *Glo.* Alack, alack, the day!
> *Lear.* When we are born, we cry, that we are come
> To this great stage of fools. *King Lear,* iv. 6.

The rounded appearance of its belly is thus described by Falstaff:

> *Fal.* My lord, I was born about three of the clock in the afternoon, with a white head, and something a round belly.
> *II. Henry IV.* i. 2.

ESTABLISHMENT OF PUBERTY: MENSTRUATION AND ITS CESSATION. The following quotations may be grouped together. In the first two the age at which puberty is established is set down as fourteen:

> I have three daughters; the eldest is eleven;
> The second, and the third, nine, and some five:
> If this prove true, they'll pay for't: by mine honour,
> I'll geld them all; fourteen they shall not see,
> To bring false generations; they are co-heirs:
> And I had rather glib myself, than they
> Should not produce fair issue. *Winter's Tale,* ii. 1.

In *Romeo and Juliet* we have a discussion as to Juliet's age, which is made out to be fourteen years all but a fortnight. Lady Capulet says:

> Nurse, come back again:
> I have remember'd me, thou's been our counsel.
> Thou know'st my daughter's of a pretty age.
>   *Nurse.* Faith, I can tell her age unto an hour.
>   *La. Cap.* She's not fourteen.
>   .   .   .   .   .   .
> Well, think on marriage now: younger than you
> Here in Verona, ladies of esteem,
> Are made already mothers.   *Romeo and Juliet*, i. 3.

In the next extract the cessation of child-bearing, as coincident with the departure of menstruation, is alluded to:

> Have we more sons? or are we like to have?
> Is not my teeming date drunk up with time?
> And wilt thou pluck my fair son from mine age,
> And rob me of a happy mother's name?
>   *Richard II.* v. 2.

The last passage makes reference to the changes of voice which take place at puberty, but which are absent in those who have been subjected to castration:

> My throat of war be turn'd,
> Which quired with my drum, into a pipe
> Small as an eunuch, or the virgin voice
> That babies lulls asleep!   *Coriolanus*, iii. 2.

SUCKLING. The two passages which follow seem to refer to the belief that the mental and moral traits of the child are influenced by the character of her who suckles the infant:

> Do as thou list.
> Thy valiantness was mine, thou suck'dst it from me:
> But owe thy pride thyself.   *Coriolanus*, iii. 2.

> He is my son, ay, and therein my shame,
> Yet from my dugs he drew not this deceit.
>   *Richard III.* ii. 2.

The following quotations refer generally to the subject:

> Wilt thou not stoop? Now cursed be the time
> Of thy nativity! I would, the milk
> Thy mother gave thee, when thou suck'dst her breast,
> Had been a little ratsbane for thy sake!
> *I. Henry VI.* v. 4.

> I have given suck: and know
> How tender 'tis to love the babe that milks me:
> I would, while it was smiling in my face,
> Have pluck'd my nipple from his boneless gums,
> And dash'd the brains out, had I so sworn, as you
> Have done to this. *Macbeth*, i. 7.

> *York.* Thou frantic woman, what dost thou make here?
> Shall thy old dugs once more a traitor rear?
> *Richard II.* v. 3.

> Here could I breathe my soul into the air,
> As mild and gentle as the cradle-babe,
> Dying with mother's dug between its lips.
> *II. Henry VI.* iii. 2.

> *Cleo.* Peace, Peace!
> Dost thou not see my baby at my breast,
> That sucks the nurse asleep?
> *Antony and Cleopatra*, v. 2.

WEANING. The weaning of Juliet, as described by the Nurse, is familiar to all readers. The points of interest in the description are the age at which she was weaned, which must have taken place when she was all but three years of age, and the mode taken to render the breast distasteful, viz., putting wormwood on the nipple:

> But, as I said,
> On Lammas-eve at night shall she be fourteen:
> That shall she, marry; I remember it well.
> 'Tis since the earthquake now eleven years;
> And she was wean'd,—I never shall forget it,—
> Of all the days of the year, upon that day;
> For I had then laid wormwood to my dug,

> Sitting in the sun under the dove-house wall,
> My lord and you were then at Mantua :—
> Nay, I do bear a brain :—but, as I said,
> When it did taste the wormwood on the nipple
> Of my dug, and felt it bitter, pretty fool!
> To see it tetchy, and fall out with the dug.
> *Romeo and Juliet*, i. 3.

CONGENITAL DEFECTS are repeatedly mentioned. *Birthmarks.* The following are allusions to birth-marks, and coupled with them we find the congenital deformities of hare-lip and squint. *Infiltration and ulceration of the cornea,* diseases most frequently found in early life, are mentioned here under the common names of "web-and-pin." This seems to have included "cataract" also (see p. 83):

> *Const.* If thou, that bid'st me be content, were grim,
> Ugly and slanderous to thy mother's womb,
> Full of unpleasing blots, and sightless stains,
> Lame, foolish, crooked, swart, prodigious,
> Patch'd with foul moles, and eye-offending marks,
> I would not care, I then would be content.
> *King John*, iii. 1.

> And the blots of nature's hand
> Shall not in their issue stand;
> Never mole, hare-lip, nor scar,
> Nor mark, prodigious, such as are
> Despised in nativity,
> Shall upon their children be.
> *Midsummer-Night's Dream*, v. 1.

> *Edg.* This is the foul fiend Flibbertigibbet: he begins at curfew and walks till the first cock; he gives the web and the pin, squints the eye, and makes the hare-lip; mildews the white wheat, and hurts the poor creature of earth. *King Lear*, iii. 4.

> Hours, minutes? noon, midnight? and all eyes blind
> With the pin-and-web, but theirs, theirs only.
> *Winter's Tale*, i. 2.

INHERITANCE OF PHYSICAL, MORAL, AND MENTAL

TRAITS. In *Winter's Tale*, Pauline, in proof of the Queen's innocence, appeals to the likeness in physical features which the babe bears to the King:

—Behold, my lords,
Although the print be little, the whole matter
And copy of the father; eye, nose, lip,
The trick of his frown, his forehead; nay, the valley,
The pretty dimples of his chin and cheek; his smiles;
The very mould and frame of hand, nail, finger:
And thou, good goddess Nature, which hast made it
So like to him that got it, if thou hast
The ordering of the mind too, 'mongst all colours
No yellow in't; lest she suspect, as he does,
Her children not her husband's!   *Winter's Tale*, ii. 3.

Timon of Athens says:

These old fellows
Have their ingratitude in them hereditary:
Their blood is caked, 'tis cold, it seldom flows.
            Timon of Athens, ii. 2.

The following lines draw a distinction between natural and acquired vices:

Lep.   I must not think there are
Evils enow to darken all his goodness:
His faults, in him, seem as the spots of heaven,
More fiery by night's blackness; hereditary,
Rather than purchased; what he cannot change,
Than what he chooses.   *Antony and Cleopatra*, i. 4.

Seb. Well; I am standing water.
Ant. I'll teach you how to flow.
Seb. Do so: to ebb,
Hereditary sloth instructs me.   *Tempest*, ii. 1.

In *Henry VI.* there is a practical advantage taken of the law:

For Henry, son unto a conqueror,
Is likely to beget more conquerors,

> If with a lady of so high resolve,
> As is fair Margaret, he be link'd in love.
>
> *I. Henry VI.* v. 5.

In the second part of *Henry the Sixth* Suffolk flings at Warwick this taunt:

> *Suf.* Blunt-witted lord, ignoble in demeanour!
> If every lady wrong'd her lord so much,
> Thy mother took into her blameful bed
> Some stern untutor'd churl, and noble stock
> Was graft with crab-tree slip; whose fruit thou art,
> And never of the Nevils' noble race.
>
> *II. Henry VI.* iii. 2.

That mental capacity does not always pass from parent to child we see in the following:

> That such a crafty devil as is his mother
> Should yield the world this ass! a woman that
> Bears all down with her brain; and this her son
> Cannot take two from twenty for his heart,
> And leave eighteen.
>
> *Cymbeline*, ii. 1.

BIBLIOGRAPHY OF SHAKESPEAREAN MEDICINE

[Some of the entries here given have not been verified. These may be found quoted in the Bibliography of the Article "Shakespeare," in the *Encycl. Britannica*, 9th edition; in the *Index-Catalogue of the Library of the Surgeon General's Office*, *U.S. Army*, under "Shakespeare," "Insanity," "Hamlet," or in the *Index Medicus*. The *British Museum Catalogue* has also been used.]

AUBERT (H. R.). Shakespeare als Mediciner. Rostock, 1873.

BEISLY (S.). Shakespeare's Garden. London, 1864.

BIANTE. Etude médico-psychologique sur Shakespeare et ses œuvres, sur l'Hamlet en particulier. *Echo Méd.* Toulouse, 1889, 2 s. iii. 52, 65, 76, 87, 99.

BIGELOW (H. R.). Hamlet's Insanity. *Chicago M. Journal*, 1873, xxx. 513.

BRADACK (F.). Shakspere on the Practice of Medicine. *Med. Rec.* New York, 1879, xv. 116.

BRIERRE DE BOISMONT (A. J. F.). Etudes psychologiques; Shakespeare, ses connaissances en aliénation mentale (Hamlet, Lear). *Annales Méd.-psychol.*, 1868, 4 s. xii. 329; 1869, 5 s. vii. 493.

BUCKNILL (J. C.). The Medical Knowledge of Shakespeare. London, 1860.

BUCKNILL (J. C.). The Psychology of Shakespeare. London, 1859.

—— Second edition, revised. The Mad Folk of Shakespeare. Psychological Essays. London, 1867. [Three of these essays appeared in *Quart. Journal Mental Science*. Reviewed in *Medico-Chirurgical Review*, vol. 26. October, 1860.]

CHESNEY (J. P.). Shakespeare as a Physician. St. Louis, 1884.

CLESS (G.). Medicinische Blumenlese aus Shakespeare. Stuttgart, 1865.

CONOLLY (JOHN). A Study of Hamlet. London, 1863.

CREIGHTON (C.). Falstaff's Death-bed. *Blackwood's Magazine*, March, 1889.

FARREN (GEORGE). Observations on . . . Rates or Laws of Mortality. . . . . Illustrations of the progress of Mania, Melancholia, Craziness, and Demonomania, as displayed in Shakespeare's characters of Lear, Hamlet, Ophelia, and Edgar; on the comparative danger of first and subsequent births, &c., &c. London, 1826.

FIELD (B. R.). Medical Thoughts of Shakespeare. Easton, Pa., 1884.

FOVILLE (A.). Les médecins dans les drames de Shakespeare. *Gaz. hebd. de méd.* Paris, 1885, 2 s. xxii. 577, 609.

GILLESPIE (J. D.). Medical Notes about Shakespere and his Times. *Edinb. Medical Journal*, 1875.

GRIFFITHS (L. M.). Shakspere and the Medical Sciences. *Bristol Med.-Chir. Journal*, 1887, v. 225-256.

GRINDON (LEO. H.). The Flora of Shakespeare. London, 1883.

HACKMAN (L. K. H.). Shakespeare and Harvey. *Lancet*, 1888, ii. 789.

HARRISON (REV. W. A.). Hamlet's Juice of Cursed Hebona. *Transactions, New Shakespeare Society*, May 12th, 1882, page 295.

HAWLEY (R. N.). The Medical Lore of Shakespeare. *Med. Age.* Detroit, 1892, x. 740-753.

HIRSCHFELD. König Lear. Danzig, 1882.

KELLOGG (A. O.). Shakespeare's Delineations of Insanity, Imbecility, and Suicide. New York, 1866.

KELLOGG (A. O.). William Shakespeare as a Physiologist and Psychologist. *Amer. Journal of Insanity.* Utica, New York, 1859-60, xvi. 129, 409.

—— Shakespeare's Delineations of Mental Imbecility as exhibited in his Fools and Clowns. *Amer. Journal of Insanity*, 1861-63, xviii. 97, 224 ; xix. 176, 322.

—— Shakespeare ; Psychological Delineations. *Amer. Journal of Insanity*, 1863-65, xx. and xxi.

—— Hamlet of Edwin Booth ; a psychological study. *Quart. Journal Psychol. Med.* New York, 1872, vi. 209.

KNOTT (JOHN). The Medical Knowledge of Shakespeare. *Medical Press and Circular*, 1892, i. 78, 101.

Lancet, October 13th, 1888. [A Leading Article on Medicine of Shakespeare.]

NICHOLSON (DR. BRINSLEY). Hamlet's Cursed Hebenon. *Transactions, New Shakespeare Society*, November 14th, 1879, page 21, see also page 218.

—— Was Hamlet Mad? *Transactions, New Shakespeare Society*, June 9th, 1882.

—— A' parted e'en just between twelve and one, e'en at the turning o' th' tyde. *Transactions, New Shakespeare Society*, November 12th, 1880, page 212.

ONIMUS (E.). La psychologie médicale dans les drames de Shakespeare. *Rev. d. deux mondes.* Paris, 1876, 3 s. xiv. 635.

OWEN (O. W.). The Medicine in Shakespeare. *Physician and Surgeon.* Detroit and Ann Arbor, 1893, xv. 289, 297.

RAY (I.). Shakespeare's Delineations of Insanity. *Amer. Journal of Insanity.* Utica, New York, 1846-47, iii. 289.

RICHARDSON (B. W.). Shakspere and the *Pia Mater*, with a note on the Originality of Harvey. *Lancet*, 1888, ii. 757. Also *Asclepiad.* London, 1888, 386-388.

RORKE (J.). Medical Quotations of Shakspeare. *West Lancet*, San Francisco. 1879-80, viii. 481, 541.

SEMPLE (R. H.). A Psychological Study of Shakespeare. *Journal Psych. Med.* London, 1881, n. s. vii. 193-210.

SIGISMUND. Die medizinische Kenntniss Shakespeares. *Cor. Bl. d. allg. ärztl. Ver. v. Thüringen.* Weimar, 1881, x. 357-367; 1882, xi. 1-17.

STEARNS (C. W.). Shakespeare's Medical Knowledge. New York, 1865.

TURNER (T. J.). The Signs of Approaching Death illustrated from Shakespeare. *Shakespeariana.* Philadelphia, 1884, i. 274-276.

WADD (W.). Commentary on Shakespeare's Medical Knowledge. *Medical Times and Gazette*, 1885, ii. 230. (Reprinted from *Brande's Quarterly Journal of Science*, No. x.)

WEST (J. F.). William Shakespeare from a Surgeon's Point of View. *Birmingham Med. Review*, 1881, n. s. iv. 265-286.

WINSLOW (F. L. S.). Psychology of Hamlet. *Journal Psychol. Med.* London, 1879, n. s. iv. 123.

WOOD (W. D.). Hamlet from a Psychological Point of View. London, 1870.

INDEX

Abortion (see also Premature birth), 100.
Abscess, 75, 79.
Abstinence, in diet, 66.
Acidity, 36.
Aconitum, 47, 52.
Aesculapius, 7.
Age, old, 39.
Ague, 17-20.
Air, in resuscitation, 72, 73.
Alcohol (see also Aqua vitae, Sherris, Infusions), 58, 59.
All's Well that Ends Well, 5, 6, 7, 31, 37, 66, 75, 76, 77.
Alopecia, 86, 90.
Amputations, 83, 84.
Antony and Cleopatra, 12, 16, 23, 38, 51, 58, 68, 73, 81, 84, 104, 108, 110.
Aphrodisiacs, 60.
Apoplexy, 7, 8, 17, 30.
Appetite, disorders of, 36; altered in pregnancy, 98, 102.
Apprehension, 33.
Aqua vitae, 47, 59.
Arrow poison, 56.
Arsenic, 53, 54.
Arteries, 14, 15.
As You Like It, 19, 37, 39.

Baldness, 86, 90.
Balsams, 47, 61.
Bagpipes, 70.
Baret, 26.
Bartholomaeus, 9.
Baths, treatment by, 92, 95.
Batman or Bateman, 10.
Bibliography of Shakespearean medicine, 113-116.
Birth (see Midwifery), premature, 98, 99.
Birth-marks, 109.
Bleeding, restraining of, 85.
Blister, 84, 85.
Blood, circulation of, 9, 10, 14.
Blood-letting, 68.
Boils, 75, 77, 78.
Boneache, 17, 30, 88, 91.
Bones, syphilis of, 91.
Boyle, Hon. Robert, 71.
Brenning, 94.
Bullein, *Bulwarke*, 95, 96, 97.
Burning and Gonorrhoea, 89, 94, 95.
"Burning Devil," 94.
"Burning" = in Hell, 95.
Butts, Dr., 5.

Caesarian section, 98, 105.

Caius, Dr. John, 3 note; 4.
Camomile, 63.
Carbuncles, 75, 77.
Cardinal Beaufort, death of, 41.
Catalepsy, 32.
Cataplasms, 47, 64.
Cataract, 83, 109.
Catarrh, 17.
Caudles, 47.
Cauterizing, 83, 84.
Cheese, and digestion, 36; and urine, 70.
Child (see Midwifery, Foetus, Deformities, etc.). New-born child's appearance and cry, 106.
Child-bearing (see Midwifery); cessation of period, 107.
Chlorosis, 17, 38.
Cicatrices, 79.
Circulation of blood, 9, 10; effect of excitement on, 34.
Civet, 47, 62.
Clysters, 47, 64.
Cob-webs, to restrain bleeding, 85.
Colic, 17, 34, 35.
Coloquintida, 47, 62.
Comedy of Errors, 6, 16, 31, 32, 43, 59, 61, 94, 105.
Congenital defects, 109.
Consumption, 17, 38.
Contagion, 22.
Convulsions, 17, 30.
Coriolanus, 8, 9, 10, 11, 21, 22, 26, 30, 35, 36, 37, 61, 65, 69, 78, 79, 84, 85, 107.
Cornea, ulcerations and opacities of, 109.
Cornelius' tub, 95.
Cotta, 4.
Counter-irritation, 69.
Cowardice, 11, 12.
Cramp, 17, 30.

Creighton, Dr. C., 26, 27, 68.
Crooke, *Microcosmographia*, 13.
Cry, new-born babe's, 106 (see also Labour).
Curare, 56.
Cures (see Therapeutics).
Cymbeline, 37, 47, 48, 49, 53, 65, 85, 92, 111.
"Cyme," 62.

Davenant's *Platonick Lover*, 95.
Death, 9; of King John, 24; of Falstaff, 25, 26; fear of, 33; in articulo mortis, 40; of Mortimer, 40; of Cardinal, 41; post-mortem appearances, 41, 42, 58.
Defects, congenital (see Deformity), 109.
Deformity of foetus, 98, 101.
Delirium, 24, 25.
Despair, 33.
Diagnosis, methods of, 42, 43, 44.
Diet, temperance in, 65; treatment of venereal disease by, 92, 96.
Digestion, disorders of, 36 (see Dyspepsia).
Diogenes and his tub for French Disease, 95.
Dislocations, 75, 79.
Dog, mad, 31.
Drink (see Alcohol), 59.
Dropsy, 17, 36, 37.
Drowning, appearances in, 42.
Dyspepsia, 31.

Ecstasy, 17, 33, 43.
Elephantiasis, 26, 27.
Empyema, 76.
Epilepsy, 17, 28, 33.
Eryngo, 60.
Esculapius, 7.
"Eugh," 57.
Evil, The, 82.
Expectoration, in diagnosis, 45.

Fainting, 73, 74.
Falstaff (as so many references occur in connection with Falstaff they have been collected here). See in Index under Apoplexy, Camomile, Consumption, Death, Drink, Dropsy, Drowning, Expectoration, Fevers, Fractures, Galen, Gout, Liver, New-born child, Pills, Pox, Purging, Quotidian, Sherris, Sweat, Urine, Venereal Diseases.
Fevers, 17, 23.
Fistula, 75.
Flax, for restraining bleeding, 85.
Foetus (see Midwifery), deformity of, 98; retained, 98; labour retarded by deformity of, 98, 101; death and retention of, 102.
Foot presentation, 98, 101.
Fractures, 75, 78.
France, malady of, 88.
French crown, 86.
French disease, 88.

Gaddesden, John of, 26, 27.
Galen, 1, 3, 6, 7, 8.
Gangrene, 75, 78.
Gerard de Narbon, 5.
Globus hystericus, 32.
Gonorrhoea, 89.
Gout, 17, 37.
Gravel, 17.
Grayness of hair, 66, 91.
Green sickness, 17, 38, 59.
Grindon's *Flora of Shakespeare*, 57.
Gums, 61.

Haemorrhage, restraining of, 85.
Hairs (see Baldness), white hairs, 66, 91.
Halliwell, 95.
Hamlet, 28, 33, 34, 39, 43, 55, 64, 79, 83, 85, 87, 93.

Harelip, 75, 83.
Harrison, Rev. W. A., 56.
Harvey, 1, 9.
Heartburn, 17, 36.
"Heben bowe," 57.
Hebenon, 47, 56.
Hebona, 56.
Heights, giddy, 34.
Hemiplegia, 17, 30.
Henbane, 56, 57.
I. Henry IV., 15, 19, 35, 36, 60, 62, 63, 67, 79.
II. Henry IV., 7, 12, 21, 22, 24, 30, 37, 38, 39, 43, 45, 52, 53, 59, 63, 65, 68, 69, 74, 78, 79, 80, 86, 93, 94, 100, 106.
Henry V., 15, 19, 22, 80, 87, 88, 92, 95.
I. Henry VI., 35, 40, 53, 78, 84, 111.
II. Henry VI., 9, 27, 30, 34, 41, 42, 74, 80, 84, 106, 108.
III. Henry VI., 61, 64, 80, 100, 101, 102, 104, 108, 111.
Henry VIII., 5, 22, 40, 65, 102, 103, 104.
Hippocrates, 7, 11.
Hope, 33.
Humours, 14, 15, 16.
Hydrocyanic acid, 55.
Hydrophobia, 17, 31.
Hyoscyamus, 56, 57.
Hysteria, 32.

Illegitimacy of birth proved by date of pregnancy, 100.
Imposthume, 17.
Incision, 83, 84.
Infection, 22.
Infusions, 47. "Hot infusions," 47, note; 60.
Inheritance, 109.
Inoculation, poison by, 56.

"Insane root," 56, 57.
Insanie, 57.
Insanity, 45 note (see Ecstasy): bibliography of Shakespearean Psychological Medicine, 113-116.
Issues, 83, 85.
Itch and Itching, 17, 37.
Jaggard, W., 13.
James I. on wounds bleeding in presence of murderer, 81.
Jaundice, 17, 35.
John: *King John*, 15, 16, 20, 23, 24, 43, 54, 55, 85, 100, 104, 109.
Joints (see Dislocation).
Jonson, Ben, 70.
Julius Caesar, 9, 18, 20, 28, 67.
King (see Lear, John, Henry, etc.).
King's Evil, 82.
Kissing, contagion by, 93, 94.

Labour, retarded, 98; premature, 98; difficult, 103.
Lancing, 84.
"Lazar-like," 28; "Lazar Kite," 92.
Leanness, 67.
Lear, 5, 11, 20, 32, 33, 34, 51, 53, 62, 77, 83, 86, 106, 109.
Leeks and wounds, 80.
Leprosy, 17, 27; leperous distilment, 28.
Lethargy, 17, 30.
Levins, 26.
Lips, contagion from, 93, 94.
Literature of Shakespearean Medicine, 113-116.
Liver, 11, 12, 13; rotten, 17.
Love's Labour's Lost, 13, 14, 15, 22, 47 note; 57, 67, 68, 86, 102.
Lowe, Peter, 83.
Lungs, rotten, 39.

Macbeth, 5, 11, 17, 18, 23, 33, 44, 51, 52, 57, 59, 62, 67, 82, 105, 108.
Madness, 45 note.
Malaria, 20, 21.
Mandragora, 47, 51.
Mandrake, 51.
Materia medica, 46.
Measles, 17, 26.
Measure for Measure, 16, 27, 29, 33, 67, 68, 73, 87, 91, 92, 93, 94, 95, 96, 97, 102, 104.
Medicine and Medical Diseases, 17.
"Medicine" and Medicines, 46.
Melancholia, 31.
Memory, ventricle of, 14.
Menstruation, beginning and end of, 106.
Mental qualities, hereditary, 111.
Merchant of Venice, 11, 13, 16, 18, 34, 66, 70, 81.
Merry Wives of Windsor, 3, note; 7, 20, 42, 60, 63, 64.
Midsummer-Night's Dream, 21, 22, 36, 63, 66, 86, 87, 109.
Midwifery, 98.
Midwives, 60.
Mixtures, 63.
Monkshood, 52.
Moral qualities, hereditary, 110, 111.
Morbilli, 26.
Morbus Gallicus, 88.
"Mother," The, 32.
Much Ado about Nothing, 15, 23, 36, 62, 104.
Murchison, Dr., 22.
Murderers and wounds bleeding, 80.
Music, in disease, 69, 72.
Musk, 47.

Naples, 86, 88 (see Neapolitan).
Narcotics, 47, 51.

INDEX

Neapolitan disease, 88 ; boneache, 88, 91.
Nervous diseases, 32.
New-born child, appearance and cry, 106.
Nicholson, Dr. Brinsley, 56.
Nodes, 90.
Non-viable period of pregnancy, 100.

Obstructions, 16, 68.
Oils, 47, 61.
Othello, 15, 16, 29, 33, 51, 53, 60, 61, 62, 64, 88, 106.
Opium, 50.

Painter's *Palace of Pleasure*, 76.
Palsy, 17, 30, 40.
Paracelsus, 1, 3, 6, 7.
Parmaceti, 47, 62.
Pathology, 9.
Pericles, 7, 38, 43, 47, 63, 65, 69, 72, 73, 88, 93, 99.
Pestilence, 17, 21 ; "red pestilence," 21.
Pharmacy, 47, 63.
Physicians in Shakespeare, 5.
Physiology, 9.
Pia mater, 13.
Pills, 47, 64.
Pin and web, 75, 83, 109.
Pinch, 6, 42.
Placket, 88.
Plagues, 17, 21 ; "red plague," 21, 22 ; plague sore, 77.
Plasters, 47, 64.
Pleura, pus in, 76.
Post mortem (see Death).
Poisons (see Toxicology), 51 ; post-mortem appearances, 58.
Poppy, 47.
Potato and "Potato-finger," 60, 61.

Potions, 47, 63.
Poultices, 47, 64.
"Powdering-tub," 92, 95, 96.
Pox, 37, 86, 87, 96.
Prawns and wounds, 80.
Pregnancy, altered appetite in, 98, 102 ; duration of, and illegitimacy and viability, 100.
Premature births (see also Abortions), 98, 99.
Presentation of foot at birth, 98, 101.
Pruritus, 37.
Psychological Medicine, Shakespearean, 45 note ; bibliography of, 113-116.
Ptisick, 38.
Puberty, date of, 106.
Pulmonary consumption, 38, 39.
Pulse, in fever, 23 ; in diagnosis, 42, 43 ; "pulsidge," 43.
Purging, 67.

Quickening, 98, 102.
Quotidian, 19.

"Radix insana," 56, 57.
Ratsbane, 47, 53, 108.
Resuscitation, from unconsciousness, 71, 72, 73, 74.
Rheumatism, 17, 20.
Rheums, 16.
Rhubarb, 47, 61, 62.
Richard II., 18, 30, 36, 57, 61, 66, 68, 69, 79, 84, 104, 105, 107, 108.
Richard III., 81, 100, 101, 107.
Richardson, Sir B. W., 13.
Rigors, 18, 23.
Romeo and Juliet, 5, 14, 33, 38, 49, 50, 52, 55, 63, 64, 69, 79, 82, 107, 109.
Rupia, 89.
Rupture, 17.

Salves, 47, 64.
Scaliger, 70.
Scars, 75, 79.
Sciatica, 17, 29.
Sea sickness, 17.
Senility, 39.
Senna, 47, 61, 62.
Serpigo, 16.
Setons, 83, 85.
Shaking palsy, 30.
Sherris, 12.
Shivering, 18, 23.
Skeat, Prof., 27.
Sleeplessness, 31.
Sleepy-drinks, 47.
Smallpox, 86.
Somnambulism, 17, 32.
Spanish sickness, 88.
Spectra, 17, 32, 57.
Spit (see Expectoration).
Squint, 75, 83.
Stars and Plagues, 22.
Strangling, post-mortem appearances in, 42.
Suckling, 98, 107, 108.
Sugar-candy, 47.
Surfeit, 65.
Surgeon, 5, 81; and venereal disease, 87.
Surgeon's box, 84.
Surgery, 75, et seq.; treatment, 83.
Sweat or Sweating sickness, 17, 27.
Sweating, treatment by, 93.
Swooning, 73.
Sympathy and sympathetic disturbance, 33.
Syphilis, 17, 86, et seq. (see Venereal disease).
Syrups, 47, 51, 61.

Taming of the Shrew, 66.
Teeth, before birth, 98, 101.
Temperance, 65.
Temperature, rise of, in fever, 24.
Tempest, 13, 19, 21, 31, 37, 39, 43, 58, 64, 110.
Tents, 83, 84.
Tertian, 19.
Tetter, 17, 28.
Therapeutics, 46, 64.
Timon of Athens, 18, 21, 27, 30, 61, 67, 84, 89, 90, 92, 94, 95, 106, 110.
Tingling, 30.
Tobacco, 57.
Touch, Royal, 82.
Toxicology, 46.
Troilus and Cressida, 12, 13, 17, 20, 23, 35, 36, 38, 40, 61, 69, 78, 79, 84, 85, 88, 91, 93, 94.
Tub, Cornelius', 95; Tub, "powdering," 92, 95, 96; "Tub of infamy," 96; "Tub-fast," 92, 95, 96, 97.
Tubs, treatment by, 92.
Twelfth Night, 5, 11, 13, 44, 60, 66,
Twin births, 98, 105.
Two Gentlemen of Verona, 44, 64.
Tympanites, 35.
Typhus, 21.

Urinal, 44.
Urine, in diagnosis, 44, 45; effect of bagpipe on, 70.
Ulcers, 82.

Variola and Variole, 26, 86.
Veins, 11, 14, 15.
Venereal diseases, 75; treated by surgeons, 88; treatment of, 92; contagion of, 93, 94.
Ventricle of memory, 13, 14.
Viability of child and date of pregnancy, 100.

Vicary, 2. *Anatomie*, 14.
Visual spectra, 17, 32.
Vital spirits, 14.
Vivisection controversy, 48.
Voice, change of, at puberty, 107.

"Wappened widow," 89.
Water (see Urine).
Weaning, 98, 108.
Wheezing lungs, 17.
Web and pin, 83, 109.

Wigs in syphilis, 90.
Wine, 12, 47.
Winter's Tale, 15, 16, 47 note: 51, 58, 60, 67, 83, 99, 106, 109, 110.
Woodall, *Obstructions*, 68.
Wolfsbane, 52.
Worms, intestinal, 35.
Wounds, 75, 79, 80, 81; Mercutio's, 82.

Yew, as poison, 56.

RETURN TO the circulation desk of any
University of California Library
or to the
NORTHERN REGIONAL LIBRARY FACILITY
Bldg. 400, Richmond Field Station
University of California
Richmond, CA 94804-4698

ALL BOOKS MAY BE RECALLED AFTER 7 DAYS
- 2-month loans may be renewed by calling (510) 642-6753
- 1-year loans may be recharged by bringing books to NRLF
- Renewals and recharges may be made 4 days prior to due date.

DUE AS STAMPED BELOW

NOV 1997

JUN 1 5 2000

12,000 (11/95)

LD 21-95m-7,'37

UNIV OF CALIF., BERK.

THE UNIVERSITY OF CALIFORNIA LIBRARY

ImTheStory.com

Personalized Classic Books in many genre's

Unique gift for kids, partners, friends, colleagues

Customize:

- Character Names
- Upload your own front/back cover images (optional)
- Inscribe a personal message/dedication on the inside page (optional)

Customize many titles Including
- Alice in Wonderland
- Romeo and Juliet
- The Wizard of Oz
- A Christmas Carol
- Dracula
- Dr. Jekyll & Mr. Hyde
- And more...

CPSIA information can be obtained
at www.ICGtesting.com
Printed in the USA
LVOW01s0312270816
502082LV00022B/246/P